BREAKING GROUND:

TEACHERS RELATE READING AND WRITING IN THE ELEMENTARY SCHOOL

Edited by: Jane Hansen/Thomas Newkirk/Donald Graves

HEINEMANN
PORTSMOUTH

HEINEMANN EDUCATIONAL BOOKS, INC.
361 Hanover Street
Portsmouth, NH 03801
Offices and agents throughout the world

First edition

10   9   8   7

ISBN 0-435-08219-1

Designed by Wladislaw Finne

Printed in the United States of America

BREAKING GROUND:

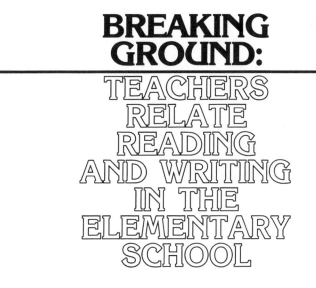

TEACHERS
RELATE
READING
AND WRITING
IN THE
ELEMENTARY
SCHOOL

Contents

Contributors

Nancie Atwell
Grade Eight English Teacher
Boothbay Region Elementary
  School
Boothbay Harbor, Maine

Carol S. Avery
Grade One Teacher
William Nitrauer School
Lancaster, Pennsylvania

Robert Bahruth
PhD Student
University of Texas,
Austin, Texas

Susan Benedict
Grade Two Teacher
Crocker Farm School
Amherst, Massachusetts

Ellen Blackburn
Grade One Teacher
Edward Devotion School
Brookline, Massachusetts

Winnifred Braun
Grade Two Teacher
Cecil Swanson School
Calgary, Alberta

Charles Chew
Chief, Bureau of English and
  Reading Education
State of New York
Albany, New York

Cora Five
Grade Five Teacher
Edgewood Elementary School
Scarsdale, New York

Alfreda Furnas
Kindergarten Teacher
York Elementary School
York, Maine

Donald H. Graves
Department of Education
University of New Hampshire
Durham, New Hampshire

Jane Hansen
Department of Education
University of New Hampshire
Durham, New Hampshire

Curtis W. Hayes
Division of Bicultural-Bilingual
  Studies
The University of Texas
San Antonio, Texas

Heather Hemming
Resource Teacher
Conrich Elementary School
Conrich, Alberta

Ruth Hubbard
Researcher
University of New Hampshire
Durham, New Hampshire

Kathy Matthews
Supervisor of Interns
University of New Hampshire
Durham, New Hampshire

Donald M. Murray
Department of English
University of New Hampshire
Durham, New Hampshire

Thomas Newkirk
Department of English
University of New Hampshire
Durham, New Hampshire

Linda Rief
Grade Seven-Eight English
    Teacher
Oyster River Middle School
Durham, New Hampshire

Martha Rosen
Librarian
Edgewood Elementary School
Scarsdale, New York

Susan Sowers
Writing Instructor
Hampden-Sydney College
Hampden-Sydney, Virginia

Janet von Reyn
Chapter I Follow Through
    Coordinator
Hopkinton, New Hampshire

Jack Wilde
Grade Five Teacher
Bernice Ray School
Hanover, New Hampshire

Acknowledgements

This book would not have been possible without the support given to research in reading and writing by the University of New Hampshire's Elliott Trust Fund. An earlier grant by the National Institute of Education was critical in initiating research in children's writing, and a teacher training grant from the National Endowment for the Humanities helped to establish a network of elementary school teachers, many of whom are represented in this volume.

In preparing the manuscript, we were helped greatly by Dori Stratton, the secretary in the Writing Process Laboratory, who worked her way through our idiosyncratic correction symbols. Linda Howe did a very careful copy-editing of the manuscript. And of course, Philippa Stratton and Tom Seavey gave us the encouragement to keep this project on track.

Preface

The three of us perused our first attempt at a table of contents in Donald Graves's study on September 27, 1984. Tom had earned the soft brown recliner. Don perched on his composition stool, twisted away from his word processor. Jane tried to think in the straight-backed, wooden, family-heirloom chair. As we scanned the list of contributors to this book, Jane noticed, "It never hit me before how many of these people are first-year teachers: von Reyn, Rief, Furnas. . . ."

"Yes, they're breaking new ground," interrupted Don as Jane continued. "Sh-h-h," he admonished. Jane glanced up and Don and Tom's eyes were locked. "We've got a title."

"BREAKING GROUND," exclaimed Tom, relieved after months of agonizing over "Understanding Reading and Writing," "Understanding Writing and Reading," "Relating Reading and Writing," "The Reading/ Writing Spiral," etc., suggestions Don Murray would toss aside as labels rather than titles.

Many of these teachers have broken new ground. They teach in environments in which they can take risks and they set up similar environments for their students. They challenge traditional expectations. They believe in what they're doing, but they're nervous. But, more important, they're also excited because their students not only learn to read and write; they like it.

New ground in writing has been broken in other books, but it's time to break new ground in reading. The philosophy behind writing process instruction is incompatible with the philosophy behind reading worksheets, tests, basals, and the fear that any deviation will endanger students' ability to learn to read. Too many students read fifty worksheets for every book they pick up. Their teachers teach what's next in the teachers' guide instead of what the students need next. Too many classrooms revolve around the teacher.

But in writing classrooms, children say, "I wrote it. I do the work." Writing teachers give students choices and listen when the children talk about what they learn. They affirm what the students know and then learn from them. Writing led many of the teachers in this book to reexamine what they did when they taught reading.

These teachers started to ask new questions, questions not typically asked about reading instruction. They were moved to publish because they had started to think more about their teaching. If they feel separated from some of their peers, at the same time, they feel closer to their students than in the past. They are all members of a literate community who write, read, and talk books.

Our book represents a teaching philosophy in which teachers expect their students to work together. Students are not segregated into proficiency groups, which reinforce social class distinctions. They are all part of the same community.

The teachers set up predictable environments in which children do as many things as possible by themselves. Janet von Reyn saw her children blossom during the month she left them alone with their writing. Carol Avery gives us a portrait of a little girl who found self-confidence when Carol assumed she could take the initiative. These teachers expect their students to make decisions, and the children do.

Freddie Furnas wondered where to start with kindergarten children. She not only helped her young students write; they surprised her and learned to read. Older students with a history of learning problems also learn to read when they enter via writing, as Curt Hayes and Robert Bahruth show us with their migrant students in Texas.

But these teachers worry. They worry about themselves, and about parents, other teachers, and administrators. They need support. Charles Chew of the New York State Department of Education encourages teachers to see parallels between reading and writing instruction. Winn Braun, a first-grade teacher, had a supportive principal who helped her convince her students' parents that their young children were learning to read. Building the parallels between reading and writing can become complicated, but Ruth Hubbard explains a framework for it. Heather Hemming elaborates on the importance of spending lots of time on reading and writing so children can talk about their own processes. One of the teachers' main questions is always: "How do I fit skills into all of this?" Jane Hansen describes some skills lessons to show how skills can be taught in the context of children's writing and reading.

Tom Newkirk and Jack Wilde show how fiction can help middle-school students explore thought and character change. Linda Rief continues with middle-school students' growth in understanding and empathy for other generations. When Linda's students presented what they learned during this unit to some teachers in a summer school writing class, they added important information about their teacher. The summer school teachers wanted to know what Rief's major role was in the unit and the students surprised both Rief and the other teachers with their answer: "She wrote, also."

Susan Benedict wrote about American history with her second-grade students as she showed how content-area reading and writing can be a way of life in classrooms. Kathy Matthews brings us into her transition classroom of children who have completed one year of first grade. These young writers use writing in all areas of the curriculum. Susan Sowers then explains the importance to first-grade children of nonnarrative writing. Cora Five and Martha Rosen share a social studies program in which students explore and write about our forefathers using their own voices.

For several years, Don Graves has been writing about the importance of "audience" to writers. He now explores the effect of an "audience" on readers. If we share what we read, we read with that other person in mind, and that person's presence affects what we think when we read. Don Murray, from whom the three of us are learning to think on paper, writes about trusting new information as it surprises us in the midst of our writing. We write to think and we read to think: this book is about thinking.

Ellen Blackburn and Nancie Atwell both show the power of literature. They persuade us that, when we talk about our writing programs, we are at the same time talking about literature. Literature is an integral part of a writing program. Nancie saw her junior-high students grow to love writing and decided to find a way to help them love reading. She found a way: her students read more than an average of twenty books a year in their English class.

In this book you will see students who want to read and write. Even more, they enjoy the challenge of good thinking. We hope you will want to make some of the teaching practices in this book your own. Enjoy the trip.

PART ONE
YOUNG CHILDREN WRITE AND READ

Stories Never End

ELLEN BLACKBURN

For three days, Shawn worked on his puppets. He drew characters from the *Ed Emberly Drawing Book of Weirdos,* glued them onto tongue depressors, and then I took them downstairs and laminated them. So far, Shawn had a devil, a goblin, a witch, and Frankenstein.

When he wasn't drawing weirdos, Shawn spent a lot of time in the listening area. One of his favorite books was *The Haunted House* by Bill Martin, Jr.

One dark and stormy night, I came upon a haunted house.
I tiptoed into the yard—No one was there.
I tiptoed onto the porch—No one was there.
I tiptoed into the house—No one was there.

In the story the character walks through all the rooms of the house and finally arrives in the attic.

I went into the attic . . .

where he is startled by his own reflection in the mirror.

I WAS THERE!

the story ends.

One day at the end of September, Shawn sat in the writing area with his puppets arranged in front of him. As he played with them he began to chant:

I came upon a haunted house.
I ooooopened the door.

Picking up his devil Shawn said,

I saw a devil!

"Hey, yeah, I can write my own haunted house book!" He did. He used his puppets as characters.

The Haunted House

by Shawn
September 29, 1983

I came upon a haunted house.
I opened the door.
I saw a goblin. A-A-A-A-A
I went in the T.V. room.
I saw a devil. A-A-A-A-A
I went in the kitchen.
I saw Daddy Frankenstein. A-A-A-A-A
I went upstairs.
I saw a witch. She went E-E-E-E-E
I thought they were bad,
but they were good.

When I started building connections between reading and writing in my first-grade classroom, I did not foresee how those connections would occur. I merely tried to narrow the gap between the children's own writing and the writing of the adult authors they read. I encouraged them to guess how professional writers found ideas for topics and how they made decisions about details, beginnings and endings. Together we speculated how a story might be changed or even how two stories could be combined.

"What if ..." I would say, "What if Hansel and Gretel met up with *The Three Robbers* in Tomi Ungerer's story?"

"Ohhh O, Ahhh!" And off we'd go.

With all of this oral rehearsal, I guess I shouldn't have been surprised when the children started to make connections in their writing. But Shawn was such an unexpected pioneer.

When Shawn had started school, only three weeks earlier, he knew six letter sounds. And, until he wrote *The Haunted House,* his longest piece of writing had thirteen words. *The Haunted House* had fifty-four words. By using Bill Martin's book as a model, Shawn pushed past his own writing limitations. He used literature to improve his writing.

Shawn built his story around the predictable sequence that Martin's book provides. All Shawn has to do is walk from room to room in the haunted house. This simple structure allows the story to move forward without a lot of organizational decision-making.

Shawn also avoids concern about sentence structure because, once again, he relies on a predictable pattern: I went in the _____. I saw a _____. He can fill in the blanks with his own places and characters. With both of these problems solved, Shawn concentrates on the production of text and adds some details of his own. Toward the end of the story he feels confident enough to deviate from his pattern, and he makes the witch talk back. Even before he had finished the story, Shawn told me: "I'm not going to have the same ending. I'm going to say: I thought they were bad but they were good."

"You don't want your story to have the same ending as Bill Martin's, do you?"

"No, 'cause everybody's heard it and if I put it the same it won't be too 'citing."

Many approaches to writing encourage the use of adult models for children's writing. Usually the model is presented several times to the children and then they are directed to write their own story based on that model. What is different in this case is that Shawn did not try to craft a piece of writing around an adult model. He chose the model because it was appropriate for the piece of writing he was conceiving. The conception of his own story came first; then he selected a model.

Shawn has many opportunities to write, and his writing is not always based on adult models. The structure of Bill Martin's story helped him, but he is not dependent on it. He selects the model which is useful to him. Other children, whose stories are offshoots of Shawn's haunted house book, also selected from their literary field.

Amy was the first child to recognize the potential Shawn's book had for her own writing. She wrote *Halloween Day* after hearing Shawn read the draft of *The Haunted House* to me. Amy doesn't need to borrow much from Shawn—just a line to use for her lead.

Halloween Day

by Amy

October 11, 1983

I tiptoed into the haunted house.
I saw a ghost. I started to cry.
I cried the whole way. I was scared.
I saw a witch. I cried even worser.
I saw a pumpkin and I felt much better.
I was laughing at him. He was funny.
I was acting like a baby.

Amy's book is actually a true account of her visit to the haunted house at the Rochester Fair. But Amy saw the relationship between her own true experience and Shawn's fictional piece and borrowed appropriately to improve her own story. Both Shawn and Amy make connections between their own activities and a piece of literature because class discussions focus on these connections.

One day after reading *The Clay Pot Boy,* the children and I made a diagram on chart paper showing all the stories the book reminded us of, (see page 7).

The children recognized four relationships among all the books: Theme, Topic, Author, and Language. At the center of the diagram are books by published adult authors, but gradually the arrows lead out to the children's own writing (set in bold type).

During the discussion the children made connections between books that were already a part of their literary tradition: books they had read, reread, listened to, or written themselves. Eventually, they began to make these connections while they were in the act of composing. This is what Shawn and Amy did. As the *Clay Pot Boy* diagram shows, the stories surrounding Shawn's haunted house book multiplied, (see page 8).

Reading the published version of Shawn's book gave Timothy the idea for *The Scarey Book*. Timothy's story is fictitious. At first he follows Shawn's model closely, and then his story takes off. Timothy is also using a segment of Mercer Mayer's book, *There's a Nightmare in My Closet,* to explain character change. The little boy in Mayer's book decides to stand up to his nightmare and shoots it with his pop-gun. To his surprise, the nightmare begins to cry. The boy's anger softens and he tucks the nightmare into bed with him. Timothy uses this same strategy to explain how he deals with one of the monsters in his haunted house.

The Scarey Book

by Timothy
October 17, 1983

I came upon a haunted house. I opened the door.
I saw a dragon. A-A-A-A-A.
I ran upstairs. I saw a goblin. A-A-A-A-A.
I jumped in the bathtub. I saw a devil. A-A-A-A-A.
and I saw blood all over him. A-A-A-A-A.
I ran upstairs. I saw Frankenstein. A-A-A-A-A.
I jumped out the window. I landed in the sea.
I saw a sea monster. I kicked him. The monster cried.
I got up. I was soaked and I felt sick.
I went home. I jumped into bed. I went to sleep.
I went back to the haunted house.
I captured the dragon. I went in the T.V. room.
I saw the goblin. I put him in the bag.
I ran upstairs and I saw the devil. I threw a bag over him. I saw

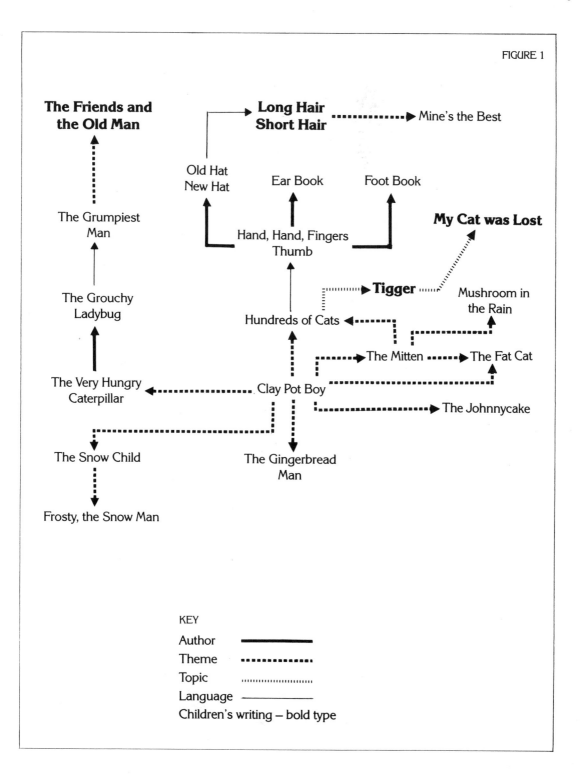

FIGURE 1

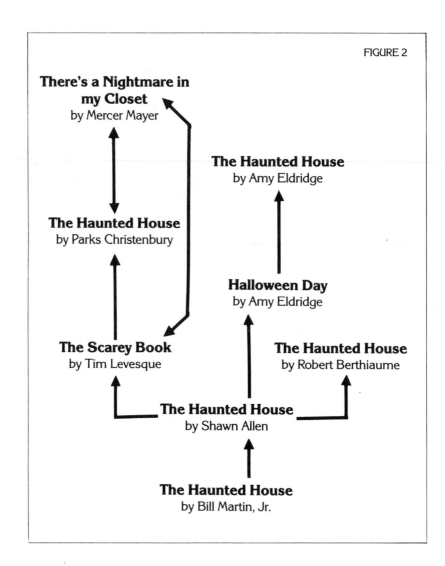

FIGURE 2

Frankenstein. I put a bag over him too. I saw the sea monster. I gave him some food. He ate it. I let the monsters go to an old castle. I took the sea monster home for my pet.

Timothy replaces the simple "I went into the _____" formula with active verbs; I ran, I jumped, I kicked, I landed, I captured. He rejects the bed-to-bed impulse. Instead he gets up in the morning, goes back to the haunted house, and takes care of the monsters one by one.

When Parks sat down to write his version of *The Haunted House,* he had a solid literary heritage to build on: *The Haunted House* by Bill Martin, Jr., *The Haunted House* by Shawn, *Halloween Day* by

Amy, *The Scarey Book* by Timothy, and *There's a Nightmare in My Closet* by Mercer Mayer. He had read and listened to Bill Martin's and Mercer Mayer's books many times. And, he had often been present while Shawn, Amy, and Timothy were composing their books. Parks's book has a more formal voice than the others. He has a better command of the language of literature.

The Haunted House

by Parks

November 8, 1983

I came upon a haunted house. I opened the door. I went in. There was a sea monster. A-A-A-A-A. I fell in. I kicked the sea monster. He cried. I felt funny. He even felt funny. He laughed and laughed and laughed. I hugged him. He felt scaley. "I'll be right back, Sea Monster. I am going to check out the haunted house." I saw a goblin. I smacked the goblin! Then the goblin smacked me in the face. I said "Nonsense!" The goblin said, "Nonsense!" Then we made up.

Me and the goblin got married. We lived happily ever after. The Sea Monster was our watch dog.

Each of the children who wrote a version of *The Haunted House* added something new to the plot. The individual authors didn't make the revisions; the story itself went through a collective revision. These revisions followed a pattern of story development often observed in the writing of individual children (Blackburn, 1982). Shawn's story relies on a formulaic structure. Amy's piece becomes a personal narrative. *The Scarey Book,* like a chain narrative, is the most expanded version. The story continues until each event is described and resolved. Of the four, Parks's story is the most focused and complete. It has elements of Timothy's story but in a compact form.

Throughout this process of collective revision, each child's story adds a dimension to the original and provides a plateau from which the next story can begin. The children don't just replicate the story, they improve it.

When children become aware of the many retellings and variations of stories that adult writers have produced over the years, they feel comfortable about experimenting within their own writing community. Another way I have found to encourage this experimentation is by writing myself and sharing these stories with the class.

I wrote *The Giant Classroom* to show the children how a writer combines truth and fiction. I wanted to encourage them to blur the edges the way Amy had in her *Halloween Day* book. The complete story is three pages long. I will excerpt parts and summarize the rest. The first paragraph is true. I used the children in my class as characters in the story.

The Giant Classroom

by Ellen Blackburn

The teacher came home from school. She was in a bad mood. All day the children in her small classroom struggled to find places to work. Robert and Eric were trying to build in the library area, but Jessica and Darcy were playing concentration in the same space. The teacher was having writing conferences. Every five minutes someone yelled, "Stop it!" "I'm telling!" "You're wrecking my house!" "Hey, you're sitting on the cards!"

In the Math Area Yudy wrote on Jaime's paper, Jaime wrote on Yudy's paper. They both started to argue. There wasn't room on the table for both papers. . . .

"Why can't I have a giant classroom?" the teacher thought. "A giant classroom." Her eyes closed. She was so tired. All of a sudden the walls began to move until it seemed they became the world all around. "That sounds familiar," the teacher thought. But, wait! It's not the world . . . it's . . . no, it can't be! But it was her classroom.

Naturally, I discover that there are some real disadvantages to having a giant classroom, especially since *everything* is giant.

In the writing area Misty and Richie were writing in their writing books. The books were as big as a parking lot. Misty and Richie jumped onto the giant stamp pad and wrote the words by walking back and forth on the page, making letters with inky footprints. "I don't know if we'll be able to publish these. Only Clifford the Big Red Dog could read them," said Richie. "Anyway, who could type on that typewriter?" said Misty.

It was true. The teacher walked over to the typewriter. It was huge. The only way she would be able to type was to jump on the keys. Well, she'd have to try, the children were working so hard. They deserved to publish their books. With all her strength she jumped on the A. Nothing happened. She tried once, twice, but still she wasn't strong enough. "Joeline! Rickie! Come and help!" All three began to jump on the key. Finally the hammer flew forward and hit the paper. The teacher was so exhausted she could hardly keep from falling. "Forget it! I can't publish any books in this classroom."

After several more adventures of a similar type, the inevitable happens, and "the teacher" wakes up from her dream.

> *The teacher opened her eyes with a start. She was sitting in her armchair. "I must have been having a nightmare! I dreamed I had a giant classroom!"*
> *The next morning when the teacher went to school she found her classroom waiting for her.*
> *And, it was still small.*

A model like this is helpful because it allows the children to follow my writing process easily. They know which parts of the story are true because they have participated in the situations I describe. They can see the seams where I have woven truth and fiction together.

My allusions to *Where the Wild Things Are* by Maurice Sendak are a more sophisticated use of literature, and the way I have used it is different from the way in which the children used the structural characteristics of Bill Martin's *The Haunted House*. They are exposed to yet another way writers borrow from each other.

Virginia Woolf once wrote:

> *Literature is no one's private ground, literature is common ground; let us trespass freely and fearlessly and find our own way for ourselves. It is thus that English literature shall survive. When commoners and outsiders make that country our own country. ...*

Children who learn to "trespass" are no longer outsiders. They are making literature their own. They are becoming members of the literate community. Stories accumulate until there is a labyrinth of intersecting stories that everyone shares.

At first, a lot of time and space has to surround the stories before the children can see the connections. Before I could make the *Clay Pot Boy* diagram I had to read many stories to the class. The children perceived these stories as self-contained entities. They needed time to think about them, time to read and reread them. When they were finally able to make connections, they could only work with stories that already existed. They couldn't yet anticipate stories that might be.

Once Shawn took that giant step and wrote his own version of an adult story, the time and distance between stories decreased. The children required less time to make connections. Relationships between their own writing and experience and the writing of others suggested themselves within a few days instead of weeks.

One day in October I read a story called "Strange Bumps" from Arnold Lobel's book *Owl at Home.* In that story, Owl is frightened by the strange bumps he sees at the foot of his bed. The bumps are really his feet, but Owl never figures this out. Several days after I read the story, Amanda stopped at the writing table.

"You know that Owl you read about?"

"The one in *Owl at Home?*"

"Yeah, well, that's just like at my house 'cause last night when I was in bed, my cat saw my feet and she thought it was a mouse."

"Your cat's like the Owl, isn't she? She thought those strange bumps were real. She thought they were mice."

"Yeah, and she tried to catch them."

Amanda held the story I read in her mind and spontaneously applied it to her own experience when she had the opportunity.

By the end of November, three months had passed since Shawn wrote *The Haunted House.* I began to see evidence that the children could hold the two processes of reading and writing together in their minds.

Robert read the class another story by Arnold Lobel. He chose "The Hat," a story in *Days with Frog and Toad.* It is Toad's birthday and Frog gives him a new hat. Unfortunately, the hat is much too big. When Toad puts it on, it covers his eyes completely. Toad is determined to wear it anyway, but when he and Frog go for a walk there are problems.

Toad tripped over a rock.
He bumped into a tree.
He fell into a hole.

The main part of the story tells how Frog solved the problem by shrinking the hat.

When Robert finished reading, he called on members of the class who wanted to comment. Over and over again the children repeated the same section of the story: "Toad tripped over a rock. He bumped into a tree. He fell into a hole." It was their favorite part. Why?

At first I was puzzled. These three little sentences were not the funniest or most interesting part of the story. Then I realized that the time/space gap had closed. The children were listening to stories and reading stories with a writer's ear, and they were fascinated by the rhythm and pattern of these sentences. I know sentences like these will appear in their writing very soon. The children have reached a turning point in their development as writers and readers. They can listen to a story and simultaneously store away words and ideas for their own writing.

In the second book of his *Lord of the Rings* trilogy J. R. R. Tolkien speaks of his conception of literature and life through his two characters, Sam Gamgee and Frodo Baggins.

Sam: *Why to think of it. We're in the same tale still! It's still going on. Don't the great tales never end?*

Frodo: *No, they never end as tales. But the people in them come and go when their part's ended.*

As the children in my class write their own stories, they have begun to recognize the relationship between their stories and the stories of other writers. They have become part of the continuous stream of stories and storytellers. As Brian told me the other day:

"You know, Ms. Blackburn, when you said that numbers never end? Well, I just noticed something. Stories never end either."

Blackburn, Ellen. "The Rhythm of Writing Development." In Thomas Newkirk and Nancie Atwell, editors, *Understanding Writing: Ways of Observing, Learning, and Teaching* (Chelmsford, MA: NEREX, Inc., 1982): 23–30.

References

2
Lori "Figures It Out": A Young Writer Learns to Read

CAROL S. AVERY

Lori was six and a half, but she was the size of a child barely turned five. The first morning she walked into the first-grade classroom she looked like a toddler lost in a department store. A tiny voice and a slight speech difficulty handicapped her first communication as she looked for her name tag amid the assortment laid out on the table. "Where's mine? I can't find mine," she implored, tears welling up in her eyes. Her name tag said "Laurencia," the name provided on the class list. We located the tag, but she looked at it with puzzlement. "What's this say?" she asked.

"It doesn't say 'Lori,'" I said. "It says 'Laurencia,'" and I explained why. Lori apparently had heard this name on occasion but had no memory of seeing it in print. She managed a smile as she put on the tag and walked away.

New situations those first few days of school often made Lori anxious and apprehensive. When we went to music class, she worried if we would come back to our classroom. At lunch she was concerned about having sufficient lunch money and finding her way back from the lunchroom. Tears came easily when situations became stressful.

During the first week of school, Lori and her classmates started writing. Lori began by drawing a stick figure surrounded by hearts and a rainbow. "That's me here," she said, pointing to the figure in the center. "These are hearts and this is a rainbow."

"Can you write those words?" I asked. "Use the letters you hear when you say the words slowly."

I went on to the next student while Lori labeled her picture with an *H* and an *R* and successfully sounded out *me* by writing ƎM.

"You wrote a word," I enthusiastically responded when I returned to her. "That's the way you spell *me*." At the same time, I wrote it without reversals and said, "This is the way it looks. We start from the left and go to the right." She was slightly disconcerted, but smiled and nodded. During the next week of school, Lori used the word *me* in her writing three times. Each time she used the left to right progression as she wrote *me,* although she frequently reversed other letters and one day wrote her name with a right to left movement: IЯO⅃.

The first-grade experience for Lori and her classmates would not be a traditional one. The writing process approach had been used in the school district for two years. My experience with it had prompted me, with administrative encouragement, to abandon the commercial reading program used throughout the district and to develop a learning process classroom in which the children's writing would be the beginning impetus and primary instrument for their instruction in learning to read. Reading and writing would be allowed to flow and develop in an interactive process, each supporting and enhancing the other. I had watched the strong effect of writing process on children's reading in previous years and marveled. The two processes seemed to go together naturally.

I spent hours setting up a classroom atmosphere conducive both to learning independently and to building a community of writers and readers. The student desks were arranged in a semicircle around a central round table that could be used for small group conferences and as a focal point for large group instruction. One corner of the room was set apart with a new beige and brown carpet. This was our reading corner, our large group sharing place. The corner looked cozy and comfortable with its pillows and shelves of books. Books were everywhere in the room. They lined the chalk railing, filled a display counter, and covered an old coffee table. Books, both by professionals and by the children, were to be an important ingredient in this language arts classroom.

I had spent much of my summer preparing for this school year. I attended writing workshops and wrote a tentative action plan for establishing the procedures and developing the atmosphere in a process-oriented classroom. I compiled a checklist of first-grade skills to ensure that my students were exposed to criteria comparable to those in the other first-grade classrooms in the school district. Throughout the year, the class would take the tests prescribed in the regular reading program to measure achievement. At year's end we would administer the California Achievement Test.

Most of the children in the class had attended kindergarten. This experience had provided them with many prereading activities, including interaction with the alphabet and an exposure to consonant sounds. Lori's achievement and ability had been assessed both formally and informally during the kindergarten year. A group-administered intelligence test placed her slightly above the mid-scale. At the end of the kindergarten year, she was reported to be grasping beginning sounds and showing an interest in words, but she was not always completing assigned tasks. My observations during the first weeks of school supported this data. She was neither a weak student nor an outstanding one. In previous years, I would have placed a child such as Lori in the middle reading group.

During the first few days of school, Lori began to relax, and during the daily writing time, she invested tremendous energy in the pictures she drew and labeled in a large journal of blank paper. She thrived on the daily responses to her efforts and the predictable schedule and environment.

There was no hurry. The time between recess and lunch, which we devoted to language arts, was relaxed and enjoyable. In those important first days and weeks we took our time—Lori, the class and I—to get to know and delight in each other. We built an accepting atmosphere. I modeled responses; the children reflected genuine, encouraging comments toward one another and one another's writing. Slowly, carefully, we put together the nuts and bolts of our classroom procedures. Nothing new was added, not even a new kind of paper, until everyone was totally comfortable with the present situation.

Each day the language arts time began with a brief lesson, which I directed to the entire group. The content depended upon developments in the children's writing that showed some were ready to learn a new concept. The focus was kept narrow. Often one child's writing was shown as an example. When several children began inserting spaces in their writing, thus breaking a long string of letters into words, I shared the accomplishment with the group and commented upon reasons for these spaces. Later in the year, these short lessons would include topics such as phonics, punctuation, and clarity of content. In the beginning, the lessons included samples of phrases and sentences from professional authors to allow these young writers to hear how good writing flows.

When the children began writing, I moved among them, listened to them read their pieces, and responded with encouraging comments. Each child began to anticipate a daily response from me. We concluded each day's writing time with a sharing time on the rug, in which two or three children presented their work to the entire group and received responses.

In a writing process classroom, it is important that writing be a part of the teacher's day as well as the student's. I kept a journal in which I recorded observations about class activities and the children's developing processes. These journal notes served as significant reflections on classroom dynamics, which helped me better understand the children and direct my teaching to their needs.

The second week of school the children wrote their first classbook, *Our Fun in the Sun.* They composed individual pages about their summer experiences, which I then typed, using correct spelling. I pasted each child's message on his/her drawing and fastened the pages in book form. The children were awed and amazed. Their words were in print! They could recall the context of what they had written that morning and were able to "read" their own writing in the published form. During the first week the children had become comfortable writing in their journals. This activity had nudged them all into something new: I urged picture labelers to try a sentence and encouraged sentence writers to expand and include more information. Every child experienced success in the process.

Lori began working on her contribution to the classbook without much involvement. She was reluctant to try this new assignment and had not progressed beyond drawing when I approached her.

"Tell me about your picture, Lori."

"Well," she slowly began, "this is me, playing, I'm outside, and this is a hill, and I'm going down this hill. . . ." Her voice drifted off.

"Oh, I see. You're playing outside and you're going down hill—this hill," I said, pointing to her picture.

"Uh huh."

"It's a big hill!" I said.

Lori smiled and nodded. I felt her gaining pride in her picture.

"Lori, I wonder, do you think you could write what you told me about the hill?" I gently asked.

"I don't know," she paused, looking intently at me. But then she picked up her pencil and began to write using her own invented spelling. Later, when she saw and read her typed words, "I am playing outside going down a hill," in the published piece, she was impressed with her accomplishment and eager for her turn to take the book home overnight.

My Journal, September 24

I am astonished at the continuing interest in our first classbook. Such a traditional topic! Yet it has had almost a magical effect in creating a group pride and an enthusiasm for reading their own and each other's writing. Over and over I hear "Read your page to me." Every night there is clamor for a turn to take the book home. Somehow that book kicked off just the right start for every one of these kids.

Reading her classmates' writing about their wide range of summer activities in *Our Fun in the Sun* provided Lori with ideas for her own writing. On the next page of her journal, Lori's drawing shows her swimming in waves at the beach. Birds fill the sky; the sun peeks in from the corner of the page. Accompanying this drawing are the first complete sentences in her journal.

I M AT TeH Bah swAwmIn I HAD A-Ge TAM
(I am at the beach swimming. I had a great time.)

Lori completely abandoned picture labeling at this point and wrote phrases and sentences thereafter.

Charlotte's Web by E. B. White was the first of many novels I read to the class. At the end of September, Lori's journal showed her involvement with the book.

TAS AI TALIS WAB WABT SAN ADRI
(This is Charlotte's Web. Wilbur standing under it.)

She shared her writing with the group that day. Her efforts delighted and inspired her peers, and in the days that followed, Lori watched several classmates write about *Charlotte's Web*. Responses to literature became frequent topics of the children's writing.

The children's rereading of their own writing became important in developing their reading skills. Initially, students did not reread what they had written and they easily forgot it. But very quickly, they realized that I expected them to read their writing back to me. Because they wanted to remember the text, they were motivated to use clues to help with the precise decoding. They knew what it meant; it was their own experience and knowledge. The challenge was to use other clues to determine the exact wording they had used when they drafted the piece. Since the children wrote as they spoke, syntax and semantic clues became natural allies as they deciphered their own writing. Using letter-sound relationships was more elusive. Some children easily incorporated this strategy, especially if they had a solid foundation in consonant sounds. Students who were shaky in letter-sound relationships or alphabet recognition had more difficulty, but still were able to use this strategy to read their writing since most consonant sounds are inherent in letter names. Writing, and reading their writing, provided children with regular practice in using all of these strategies (Bissex, 1980).

From the first day of school I read to the class at least twice a day. We started each day with a chapter from a children's novel. *Charlotte's Web* was the first of ten novels we enjoyed. Later in the morning, and again when time permitted at the end of the day, we read picture books, poetry, or books related to the science and social studies areas of the curriculum. Always we read to enjoy the rhythm of language and understand the communication of the author. We discussed authors, compared styles of writing, and explored unknown vocabulary in the context of the writing.

By mid-October the children were easily reading their own writing to others and were becoming keenly interested in trade books. We began to devote five minutes several times throughout the day to "read" books. I moved among the children, conferring with them just as I had been doing during writing time. They talked about the pictures and the storyline, and pointed to a few words they recognized.

Again, Lori was confused and anxious. "I don't get it. How do I read this book?" she would ask. When I suggested she look at the pictures and read the story that way, she said, "Yeah, but what about the words? I don't know how to figure the words out." (How to "figure it out" was a phrase that Lori used throughout the year.) Lori then discovered a book in the classroom entitled *Cats and Kittens*. It pleased her because she owned a cat. The brief text was illustrated with many photographs. She determined the word *cat* by using the initial consonant, *c*, and the picture of a cat on the page. Once her conclusion was verified as correct, she settled back to spend several days with the book.

Lori did not always understand initially but she possessed determination and spunk, and a strong desire to learn. She never doubted that she would conquer the printed word. For Lori, it was a question of when and how, of "figuring it out." What was the key to unlocking this code?

My Journal, October 19

I feel a tension and a tremendous energy in these children working so hard at their reading. There is such an outpouring of effort and strength! At the same time I feel a vulnerability; this is really high-risk activity. I think I function best when I help maintain the atmosphere, remind them of all the strategies they could use and then step back. As I move among them, answering their questions and responding to their successes, I sometimes feel I'm an intruder. There's a danger that I might throw them off by asking them to deal with my *priorities and I know that would be a mistake at this point. No schooling prepared me for the powerful unfolding that is taking place around me.*

Writing with her own invented spelling reinforced and expanded Lori's knowledge of letter-sound relationships. She now wrote several letters in succession to form words. *FLAW* stood for flower; *san* for sun; *Pamn* for Pac-man. This task was not difficult for her; her auditory discrimination was keen and her memory excellent. The regular practice through daily writing developed both her auditory and visual skills. As she wrote, she became aware not only of the use of phonics, but of a visual approximation of the word she was writing.

The stage was set for Lori to read. With great delight, she began applying strategies she had devised when writing to decode words in other print materials. "This book's a bit hard for me to read," she began one day, and then added brightly, "But I can read *of* because I already knowed that word." A few days later Lori found the word *flower* in a book. "Does this say *flower*?" she asked me. I nodded. "I thought so. You know why? 'Cause I remembered those letters were in *flower* from when I did my writing." Another day she said, "I found the word *go* and the word *the.*" It was a large step. She was overcoming her bafflement of print. Her confidence expanded; she was learning to read!

By the end of October, Lori was using the sight words she had acquired from her writing, consonant sounds to attack words she didn't know, picture and context clues, and her memory of the text to read a complete book, *Rosie's Walk* by Pat Hutchins. Lori was interested in the book because I had read it to the class earlier. She spent five days mastering it and came to me, eager to share her accomplishment. As she read, she was highly involved with the text and stopped to elaborate on the story line with observations of the pictures. Independently, Lori had decoded and then memorized the text, and although she did not know many of the words in isolation, the context provided support for accurate decoding. It was the context and reading for meaning that were important to her. She had successfully transferred to this task her accumulated knowledge of written language and the decoding strategies she had used when she read her own writing (Bissex, 1980).

When she finished the book, she looked at me and smiled. I smiled and nodded in acknowledgment. She did not need praise; the learning had brought its own reward. "What will you read next?" I asked.

"I don't really know yet," she replied, "I think I'll go look for something."

The confidence and determination Lori possessed by this time were demonstrated at the class Halloween party. After several classmates had unsuccessfully bobbed for apples and given up, Lori plunged in, and on her first attempt came out with an apple clenched in her jaws, despite the fact that she was currently missing two front teeth! How different from the cautious, tearful child of September.

Lori had cracked the code. She tore into reading materials and, in November, read eleven separate titles to me. She selected what she read herself and quickly learned what was too hard. Usually she chose materials in which she knew some words and used context and graphic clues to decode the rest. One day in early December she brought a small paper book to me and said with amazement and elation, "I just picked this book and I can read it all! I didn't have to figure out any of the words 'cause I knowed them all already!"

My Journal, November 29

In the last month I have felt my class, one by one, cross an important initial hurdle. Their decoding strategies and the sight words learned from their writing have enabled them to cut through the mystery of print in trade books in the room. They miss words here and there but they can decipher enough to put the meaning together. I rejoice with them. They're on their way!

From the first day, my responses to the children's writing began with a positive acknowledgment of content and then an expression of my interest in learning more about their topics (Graves, 1983). That response almost always had the intended effect: to prompt the child's thinking about expanding the writing, and to give total responsibility for that decision to the child. Often, in writing conferences, I would ask "What do you plan to do next?" Eventually, the children anticipated that question, began to think through the answer, and already had tentative plans for revision. The dialogue of the writing conference helped them verbalize their thoughts. They came to accept that their initial drafts need not be perfect or finished products. When the children became able to work independently during writing time, I often participated in class activities as a writer and allowed the children to observe my drafts in various stages. This modeling of the process was an important element in the children's willingness to struggle with revisions.

The group sharing time had an established format. The author read his or her piece and called upon peers for comments. Our rules called for saying first what one liked about the piece as specifically as possible, and then asking questions about clarity. The questions the children asked were modeled on those they had heard me ask both in these sessions and in individual conferences. The atmosphere we created for sharing our writing was significant. A trusting environment allowed for the risk-taking that would be the basis for process learning.

During writing time one day in November, Lori read her piece to the class.

When I Went on the Bike Path

I am with my Mom on the cemetery grass. We are going on the bike path now. This is the Farm Museum Property. They have very much property. I am getting tired now. I saw a blue jay. I found a bench. I was very happy. I sat down. I slept for a while. Then I woke up. Then I walked again.

When she finished, Marlene responded, "I like the property part."

"The farm museum property. They *do* have very much property," Lori confirmed.

"I like the word *property,*" replied Marlene. "It sounds good there."

Jason hesitantly commented, "I was sorta confused about the blue jay. You said you were tired, and then you said how you saw a blue jay and then you said you sat on a bench." The confidence on Lori's face began to fade. She said nothing.

"What happened to the blue jay?" asked Danny.

Somewhat teary-eyed, Lori defended her piece. "Nothing more happened. That's all." The class accepted Lori's answer.

"I think it's a good piece," proclaimed Jenny.

A few minutes later Lori took a new sheet of paper and wrote: *The blue jay flew and flew.* She took the staple remover, pulled out the staples, inserted the new page in proper sequence, and restapled the booklet. Later that morning, when she shared her addition in large group sharing time, she received many favorable comments.

The risk Lori took in sharing her writing, together with her interaction with the class, resulted in a big step in her development as a learner. Her writing fluency increased and at the same time, she became a more critical reader of her own writing. When she wrote *Me and Fish,* she was highly motivated to tell her story and to include *all* the details she could recall.

As Lori's writing progressed so did her reading. When she read *It Didn't Frighten Me,* a book with a repetitious word pattern, she commented, "This book was easy. Know why? 'Cause it says the same thing over and over so when I figured it out once I could just read it again." Each time she read the repeating phrase, "It didn't frighten me!" she added a new degree of expression to her voice. Occasionally she picked up a book that she had abandoned earlier and now found she could read it. There was surprise and delight when she reported, "I couldn't read this before when I tried, but now I can."

The addition of child-authored books to the classroom library provided Lori with an abundance of new reading materials that were easy to master because of their familiar context and language. On a daily basis, she chose one and read it to the author, the *authority* on the book. The author was responsible for teaching the readers and assisting them through any difficulties. When a child read a book to the author's satisfaction, the reader signed the card in the back and took the book home overnight. Throughout the year, the growing collection of peer-authored books was acknowledged by all the children to be the "best" books. Lori said they were "the most fun books 'cause you know the author."

Lori's growing reading experiences expanded her writing. In December she wrote about the approaching holiday.

To Nite its Christmas eve Santa is going down the chimney evin
We dont have a chimney But he cAn get in WetH his Key

When I noted her improved writing vocabulary during a conference, she told me, "Since I been getting into reading I remember words I seen when I was reading so then I can write them." She noticed quotation marks when she read and began using them in her writing. She was obviously ready to learn this skill, so I instructed her in the proper use of quotation marks and helped her apply them. By mid-January Lori could correctly use quotation marks and explained them to another student.

In mid-December the class took the Level 2 test of the district reading program (Level 1, a reading readiness level, was omitted).* A score of 45 was considered passing. The range in the class was 46 to 50, and nine students, including Lori, scored a perfect 50. During my years of teaching the reading program, I had never had everyone in the class take the test before Christmas and occasionally scores had dipped to the low 40's. The results of the test reassured both me and the school administrators of the success of these young readers. The more important feedback about their reading progress came from my daily interactions with their reading process.

By this time the children were able to sustain longer stretches of reading time and the short periods had been consolidated. I used the skills checklist and my observations of the class' achievement to select reading strategies and skills to present in daily lessons. The children readily applied these to their reading. It was usual to hear comments such as: "I found a word that has *ea*. I can sound it out."

I had brief reading conferences with most of the children daily. Children read a sentence or two of a book to me and commented on the piece, or asked assistance with comprehension problems or decoding struggles they were having. I listened to individuals and small random groups read and discuss entire selections. I recorded anecdotal comments on student progress in the reading folder I kept for each child.

Lori's reading and writing continued to be strong after Christmas. The first week back from Christmas vacation she read *The Giving Tree* by Shel Silverstein, which I had read to the class just before we departed for the holidays. "Did anything give you trouble when you read this?" I asked.

"Yeah, I had a bit of trouble with a few words like 'carried' and 'whispered,' but I just remembered them from when you read this book to us so then I could read them."

Lori tackled longer and more difficult reading texts, including Arnold Lobel's *Owl at Home*. She admitted that "there's some words here I

*This refers to the End-of-Level Test of the Scott, Foresman and Company Unlimited Reading Program c. 1976. Levels 1–4 of this program are designated for first grade. In a typical class, it is possible that a few students may complete Level 5, and some students will go only as far as Level 3 in first grade.

don't know. It's pretty long. But I like owls, so I really want to read this book."

During this period Lori wrote with ease. She was never at a loss for topics. Her invented spelling and sight words for writing were accomplished enough to permit fluency. She published *Penguins,* inspired by *Mr. Popper's Penguins* which I had read to the class. Her book recounted all the factual knowledge she had learned about penguins, a topic in which she developed a special interest. Her parents bought her a stuffed penguin and a shirt with penguins on it.

My Journal, January 26

Teachers observing in the classroom today asked questions that I'm asked a lot. They see kids writing or reading and note the wide range of activity with everyone working on task. "How do you get kids to do this? How did you get to this point?" they ask. I think the answer is time and atmosphere. I am so glad that I took time in the beginning to establish the structure. Now so much is happening all around me. The classroom is relaxed and trusting—and busy. One visitor described it as a cocoon where metamorphosis is taking place.

During the late winter months, writing and reading flourished in the classroom. The children's writing topics expanded and distinctive styles began to emerge. The books the children read, as well as those read to them, contributed to improved sentence structure and vocabulary. Some children wrote fiction using characters from favorite books. All of them became enchanted with dedications, author's pages, tables of contents, and chapters, and these techniques appeared in child-authored books. I found it important to repeat many previously introduced concepts as children became receptive to learning new strategies or mechanical skills. Repetition offered reinforcement for some students and opened new avenues to other children who, for one reason or another, had not been ready to understand a concept previously.

Earlier in the year the children often read only parts of stories, but now they read entire trade books, an assortment of basal readers and, especially, peer-authored materials. I noticed a difference in the reading approach of this class which I had not seen in previous nonwriting first graders. As readers, they were far more aggressive and critical, striving continuously for content. I believe this attitude grew out of reading their own writing and, therefore, out of their basic understanding that writing holds meaning to be conveyed to an audience (Chomsky, 1979).

As the year progressed, the spread in achievement levels became greater and learning strategies became more diverse. The strongest students, of course, quickly assimilated a broad range of strategies. The use of phonics was an important strategy for some students but insignificant for others. Vowel sounds were difficult for some because of what appeared to be developmental reasons, but those children became good readers by using other strategies that worked for them, such as sight words and context.

The progress of every child was not steady. Sometimes reading and writing interest and growth raced ahead; at other times they leveled off for several weeks or even declined slightly (Graves, 1983). I resisted the temptation to push a child who was struggling and trusted that the learning process was working even though I could not see it.

In March, Lori's learning patterns changed. Her fluency in writing dropped. She began several pieces that she never completed. "I don't like this writing. It doesn't sound so good to me." Or, "I just don't know what else to write. I know what happened but I don't want to put that in." She continued to read steadily but chose mostly to re-read many books that she had read before. At the same time, vowel sounds were being emphasized in the classroom instruction and Lori appeared to be incorporating these into her reading strategies. She re-read Arnold Lobel's *Days with Frog and Toad* and announced, "I couldn't read all the words here before but this time the only thing I had trouble with was *pocket.* All I had to do was sound that out."

Toward the end of April, Lori appeared to begin pulling out of her slump. She decided to write another book about penguins to include all the new information she had learned. She dedicated it to "Penguin Lovers" and at the end, on her own initiative, included the following author's message:

Athers Messgs

I thot of writig Penguins by looking it up in a Book. this is the Secnit Penguin Book   Do You Know Why: Because I Know a lot More abot Penguins

Lori's classmates loved this book, and its popularity and success marked a resurgence in Lori's learning which continued until the end of the year. She completed several pieces of writing begun earlier and expanded her reading interests.

My Journal, April 19

These kids are deeply involved with reading and writing and at the same time encouraging each other. They've formed a supportive, caring community! It's an environment that encourages risk, and risk-taking seems to be a key for them. To maximize their learning in this environment, I think it's important for me to keep my focus on the kids and to listen—really listen—to them. Then they can show me where they are and what they need and I can respond in ways to continually nudge and stimulate their growth.

Throughout the year the class had continued to do well on the periodic reading tests of the school district's reading program, indicating that their achievement level matched that of their peers in the other first grades. Lori had achieved a perfect 50 on all three of these tests. In late May the reading portion for first grade of the California Achievement Tests was given to the class. The test consisted of three parts: phonic analysis, reading vocabulary, and reading comprehension. Lori scored a 93 percentile with a grade level assessment of 2.8. The class range on this test was 76 percentile to 99 percentile. Four children in the class completed perfect test papers and scored 99.

The test demonstrated Lori's strong achievement level, but it did not indicate the kind of learner she had become. She exuded confidence and enthusiasm during the last weeks of school. She struggled for clarity as she wrote her final piece of the year, *The Dog and the Cat,* in which she attempted for the first time to write fiction. She shared the piece many times and used group interaction to give her direction in revising for meaning. When it was finished, she declared it the best piece she had ever written because "it's so long."

She had become an avid reader and told me with delight and satisfaction one day, "I really like to read *Charlotte's Web.* I can read it now, the whole way through, without any struggling."

I interviewed Lori in June regarding her learning processes. Her comments about writing revealed her current concern for correct spelling and her procedures for dealing with this problem.

You see, when you sound out words you just can't always get it right. Like 'have.' You sound it out and you put 'hav' and figure out there was an 'e' at the end. You have to remember which ones do that. ... Now say I was spelling dinosaur. That would be a hard word to spell and I only could get a couple letters down and then you look it up in a book. When I looked it up I remembered I know how to spell it 'cause I remembered how to spell 'penguins' that way.

When asked how she learned to read, her very direct reply was: "By reading more books and more books and more books."

"What do you do with words you don't know?" I asked. "I just figure out myself," she answered.

Lori has assumed responsibility for and control of her own learning process. She has invested herself in learning and discovered its intrinsic rewards. Like her classmates, she is not hampered by the fear of failure. Lori is a risk-taker, eager to meet the continuing challenges of learning.

References   Bissex, Glenda L. *GNYS AT WRK: A Child Learns to Write and Read.* Cambridge: Harvard University Press, 1980.

Chomsky, Carol. "Approaching Reading Through Inventive Spelling." In *Theory and Practice of Early Reading,* vol. 2. ed. L. B. Resnick and P. A. Weaver. Hillsdale, N. J.: Lawrence Erlbaum, 1979.

Graves, Donald H. *Writing: Teachers and Children at Work.* Exeter, New Hampshire: Heinemann Educational Books, 1983.

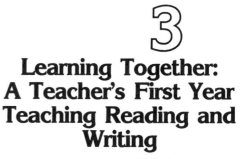

3

Learning Together: A Teacher's First Year Teaching Reading and Writing

JANET VON REYN

Looking back, I see that Kristin and I had a lot in common. It was my first year teaching school. It was Kristin's first year in school. I know I had all the anxieties and insecurities common to first-year teachers. And I imagine that Kristin had her own share of these feelings. My first impression of her was of a shy, pale child half-hidden in her mother's skirts. She shadowed me during those early days, looking to me for guidance in most matters. In a routine assessment, she knew her alphabet and most of the consonant sounds, but she was not reading. A quiet child, she didn't stand out in my mind.

Through the writing process, Kristin and I have both come a long way from those uncertain beginnings. Kristin writes and publishes stories, which she reads to her classmates in a clear, proud voice. As for me, I have learned that writing can play an instrumental part in teaching children to read. Kristin, for example, can read at or beyond the second semester level of first grade. How did this happen?

I didn't set out to teach my twenty kindergarteners how to read. I was a first-year teacher and I wanted to run a writing program. That seemed enough of a challenge.

My own views about teaching reading in kindergarten were confused. Part of me, the part that was trained in the early seventies at a progressive school, felt that young children should not be forced into systematic instruction, but should be allowed to make their own choices from a range of activity centers. This view is based on faith in the young child's strong desire to learn, and in play as the way in which young children learn. It is also based on an appreciation of the individual needs and interests of each child.

Part of me knew that some children began to read even before they reached school. Usually their parents, loath to seem pushy, quickly said, "He learned on his own. We didn't teach him." So some children, at least, were not too young to learn to read at age five.

Then there was a part of me symbolized by the floor-to-ceiling gray metal cabinet that loomed hugely in the corner of the room. The shelves were crammed with stacks of materials from the reading programs of former kindergarten teachers. These workbooks, dittos, and suggestions for cute ideas to teach letters became unwelcome reminders of the ways in which my predecessors had fulfilled their teaching responsibilities. They were experienced teachers and they had used all this. Who was I to turn my back on it? Well, I rationalized every time I closed the doors after a session of self-torture spent paging through these materials, I can't do *everything.*

I began our writing program before school opened by inviting the children, in groups of six or seven, to come to school with their parents. While the children played, I helped the parents make a book for their child. I asked each parent to inscribe a message in the child's book. Then, on the first day of school, the children came to a room they had seen, and a teacher they had met. On the tables were the big (9″ × 12″) journals their parents had made. As the children colored on the covers and wrote their names, I sensed that an early connection between home and school had begun through books and writing.

On the second day, we began the routine that continued throughout the year. During the fifteen to twenty minute worktime preceding free choice, I assigned four or five children to the writing table. No one balked, and most were eager. The rest of the class was divided into groups of four or five to do math, science, or art activities. Since I taught alone, I tried to make these other activities self-directed, but this was not always possible. Nevertheless, I tried to station myself at the writing table. It was where I liked to be the most.

"You can write in your books now" was all I had to say and they began to draw. Only Kristin, who joined our class in early October and who had gone to an "academic" kindergarten, looked doubtful the first day she wrote. "I don't know how to write." "Oh, but you draw pictures. That's writing, too." From the beginning, I included drawing when I spoke of writing. Drawing pictures was a way of putting a message on a page. For kindergarteners the pictures told the story, and many continued to feel that print was an unessential embellishment.

Because I was using the writing program in place of a conventional reading program, I asked each child to write one or more words to accompany his drawing. I wanted them to learn to sound out and write words. I was as eager for those early scrawls as a mother is for her child's first words. We chose a word with strong phonics to sound out. The child wrote what he could hear, e.g., RKT (rocket). The alphabet hung near the writing table and children consulted it and one another for help in recognizing and writing letters.

They were getting as much, if not more, practice with phonics than they would with our basal reading program. The writing table often sounded like some kind of phonics-powered machine, as each child labored to sound out words: "ssss pppp rrr mmm nnn—superman!"

From the beginning, phonics and other conventions of print (e.g., spaces between words, writing horizontally across the page) were important tools, but ones which were subordinate to getting the meaning down on the page. This meant that children gained word analysis skills while never losing sight of the most essential part of any reading program, namely, that reading conveys meaning.

Kristin's first drawing (October 6) showed a person under a rainbow. She drew flowers on the bottom of the page. She told me, "This is me when I was looking at the rainbow. The rain made the flowers grow." Her next entries showed carefully drawn houses and rainbows. By October 20, she had begun to draw more quickly, using larger strokes and a scribbling effect. I think she became freer as she realized this was her own book, and that she could do whatever she wanted in it. She wrote her first word: SOM (sun). My usual way of responding to children's writing was to tell what I saw and then ask them to tell me about their writing. I tried to write down what they said in clear capital letters, thinking it would be easier for them to read when they were ready to try, even though there wasn't always space on the page. In another entry on October 20, Kristin copied the name of a friend in the space below where I had written it after she talked about her writing.

A week later her journal entry showed a small rainbow and sun but also two new additions to her repertoire: a friendly looking witch and a ghost. These would reappear when she began to write stories.

On December 12, Kristin drew a two-page spread with a picture of a person on one page and a house on the other. As usual, I sat close to her expecting her to tell me about her writing and sound out a word or two. After I wrote *This* she took the pencil out of my hand and sounded out: LADYYNT TO THAP TO GT CM MLK (Lady went to the A & P to get some milk). On the next page was the by now familiar house. She explained, "She left her kid at home." I wrote down her first words and she wrote HOM. This was the beginning of a favorite topic for Kristin, namely, little girls who are left behind. This evolved into an interest in little girls that had problems with queens and witches, who tried to, and sometimes did, kill them, e.g., "The-Wicidgoenkilldthe girl." (The wicked queen killed the girl.)

From mid-December to early February, Kristin was content to draw pictures with no print, although she was interested in writing words if I worked with her. At this point, print did not seem important to her. However, I did not respond consistently and thoroughly to her drawings. I suspect Kristin and other children might have shown more progress towards reading if they'd had regular conferences to encourage and help them write.

During January and the beginning of February I couldn't see the progress many of the children were making in their writing, and my "gray-cabinet anxiety" reasserted itself. Throughout these six weeks or so, I tried to run, simultaneously, a reading group using workbooks, a writing group which was self-directed, a math group, and an art activity. It was hard to accomplish all of this in a satisfying way, and I felt torn. I still sensed that I was doing the right thing in writing; but I also wanted the reassurance a systematic reading program seemed to offer.

The irony was that during the period when I was plagued with doubts about relying on the writing program, and had turned my attention toward a conventional workbook approach, Kristin and her classmates were making important progress. There came a day in early February that I remember well. Kristin came up to me and showed me her journal. There in big bold letters was: This Si A GRL ANDSHE SI HVING ANISKREM. (This is a girl and she is having an ice cream.) I looked down at her in amazement. "Kristin, you wrote that all by yourself!" I was so excited. Moments later another child, Christie, came up and showed me her journal. To my knowledge, she had not written on her own either and yet here was: THE IS A MOV (This is a movie.), THES PAEL (These are people), THE IS E.T. (This is E.T.) They were both grinning. "Christie you can write!" As I hugged her and held her solid, chunky little body, I recalled that she had told me glumly, back in October, "All I can make are houses." As we had paged through her previous entries, we had come upon some trucks she had drawn. Her face had lit up and she had gone on to draw a TV—a task she felt she couldn't do until she had reviewed past accomplishments. Her increasing sense of competence was serving her well in her new venture as a writer.

As I let the children know how excited and proud I was of their achievement, I felt a little like a mother whose baby has taken a first step while she was looking the other way. I had missed a big moment, but there would be other big moments. I decided to quietly put the workbooks away and return to the writing table, where I'd wanted to be all along.

After Kristin's breakthrough in early February she began to write almost daily, sometimes making single entries, going back to add words to earlier drawings, or writing stories. She also chose to spend time in our classroom library, reading books. In May, I asked her to stay after school one day so I could find out how writing might have helped her learn to read.

I asked her, "Do you think writing helps you to be a better reader?"

"Yes."

"Why?"

"Because I write my own writing and I know what that says."

By writing her own story, Kristin already comprehends the meaning of the words. She doesn't have to cope with the double task of sounding out or identifying words, and then making them add up to some unknown message. It's the difference between doing two kinds of puzzles—one that provides an overall outline of the picture to be made and another that is just a pile of pieces. Writing helps make reading a deductive process: the child knows the general idea and needs only to identify the parts that must be there. This seems easier than the inductive process: figuring out tiny parts to make a word and then stringing the words together to discover the unknown meaning. The child doesn't have to construct meaning at the same time she's working on breaking the code of print.

I asked Kristin to choose a book from our library that she didn't know how to read, and she brought *Animal Babies.* I watched her as she opened to the first page. First she looked briefly at the picture and then at the words. She read along slowly and smoothly. When she came to one she didn't recognize, she tried to sound it out. She would have a little question in her voice as she did this. When she got the word right, I murmured agreement and she went on. If she couldn't sound it out, she looked at the picture for clues.

I asked her, "What do you do when you read?"

"I sound it out."

"And if that doesn't work?"

"Then I make up a word."

Of course, she is used to making up words from her own writing. So here, she substitutes a word that fits into the meaning she's been constructing.

She came to "small game" and didn't know the words. "*Smell?* No, No. If it had a K it would've been *smack.* If I figure out this one (game) maybe I'll figure this one (small). If this was a J it would be *jam* but that doesn't make sense." She is constantly trying to "make sense," to get the whole idea. She worked for several minutes, without becoming frustrated, but also without figuring out the words. She didn't know the other meaning of the word "game" (as in "hunting small game") so she had the double task of constructing meaning while sounding out the word.

I asked Kristin to get me her published book, *Poochie and the Wich.* The published books had the children's original illustrations and invented spellings because I found the boys and girls unwilling to re-illustrate their stories for publication. I typed the conventional spelling below theirs.

Some children, like Cynthia, found it easier to read their own writing but I asked Kristin which was easier for her to read. She answered, "The typing because I think some of my writing is wrong and yours is right." Kristin is further along the reading path than Cynthia, and she chooses to read the typing "because then you read the right thing."

We then paged through her journal and came to an entry from the end of March. She had written: THAS IS TEDEA and Tana GATG UP

(This is Teddy and Tana getting up). She had trouble reading TEDEA but was able to sound it out. "Why did I write an *A* at the end?"

"How would you do it now?"

"TEDIE."

Kristin has moved far beyond what she understood about writing and reading when she entered school. Just as important, if not more so, is the pleasure and self-confidence she exudes about school in general, and writing and reading in particular. The little girl who hung about me looking for direction has now written many stories and announces, "I can read seven books."

I had to smile when, with new-found cockiness, she answered my question, "Can you write anything you want to?"

"Yes."

"Do you need to know anything to be a better reader?"

"No."

A while back I sat in Jane Hansen's office wondering at Kristin's progress. I was as quick as a parent to say, "But I didn't teach her to read."

Jane's eyebrows shot up. "Of course you did. Maybe we just have to redefine what we mean by teaching." Maybe we do.

At this point, it's hard to make a completely accurate assessment of the contribution the writing process made to Kristin's reading. Maybe she would have come as far on her own at home, although her mother told me she believes Kristin learned to read in kindergarten.

I do know that she and the other children, through their writing, learned how to sound out and write words. More importantly, they learned to convey meaning through their drawings and words.

We know young children learn through play. They explore, invent, and practice in their drive to know and master their world. Why should they approach beginning reading any differently? A kindergarten writing program can become yet another activity that engages a young child as totally as blocks, sand, and water, and allows her to play her way into reading.

As for me, I've come a long way, too, from the anxious first-time teacher haunted by a monster gray cabinet. Kristin and her classmates have taught me a lot about teaching beginning writing and reading. It can be accomplished without a systematic reading program, which can pressure the teacher into trying to "cover" all aspects of the program. All the paraphernalia of workbooks and dittos can end up coming between the teacher and child, making the process of learning to read needlessly encumbered.

In a busy classroom, writing was often the only time I spent with one child alone. Looking into her face, admiring her writing, being there to listen and to help allowed me to get to know each child. At writing, at sharing, and at story time, they came to know me—as a person who loved their writing and reading and books. If the enthusiasm and self-confidence of Kristin and the other children about writing and reading are any indication, then perhaps I have been their reading-mother, passing on to them my growing love and understanding of writing and reading, and my confidence in their ability.

I asked Cynthia, a serious artist who likes to get everything right, "When you pick up a new book, do you think you'll be able to read it?"

"Well, I'm not really sure but I have some courage."

Maybe that's the best part—that Cynthia, Christie, Kristin, and the rest of the children, as well as their teacher, have "some courage" now—as writers and readers.

Watch Me

ALFREDA FURNAS

A small voice calls out excitedly from the quiet of the darkened room, "I know what that says!" I look up from my writing to seek the source of the voice. In the glow of the overhead projector, I can see Janice's hand waving, her five-year-old face triumphant. I have written, "Tomorrow we are going to the duck pond." She can read it. I am as delighted as she is. Janice has been writing with invented spelling for months. Recently she has been able to write without assistance. It now appears that she has begun to read as well.

Although it is considered unusual at the kindergarten level, I had chosen to teach my students writing for several reasons: 1) through my study of writing process, I knew very young children could learn to write and enjoy it; 2) the establishment of writing process was being encouraged throughout the school system; and 3) making a writing process program part of the curriculum at any grade level offers a unique opportunity for individual growth and advancement.

I read Glenda Bissex's book, *GNYS AT WRK* (1980), and was sure that my kindergarten children could learn to be writers with as much ease and delight as had my third-graders the year before. I knew I was in trouble however, when at the beginning of the year, I began to introduce writing by asking the children to write their names at the top of a piece of paper. Only half of them picked up their pencils. Jesse's eyes filled with tears for the third time that day, and Ben blurted out, "I donna how to write my name."

I had forgotten. I had forgotten that kindergarten students, for the most part, would have had little experience with writing, that over half would not know their alphabet, and the majority would know few if any letter-sound associations. I realized, at once, why teaching writing to kindergarten children is viewed by many as impossible. They need to learn so much of what is basic to the process of writing. They need to learn letter-sound associations. They need to be able to recall letter shapes and reproduce them from memory. They understand that people write things having meaning and that the written things can be read; but they, for the most part, do not understand the concept of putting thoughts into words, words into sounds, sounds into letters, and then letters into words. Further, even when they understand the process of writing, it is hard for them to understand that what has been written can then be unscrambled—read—in much the same manner.

Although still hopeful that it could be done, I was overwhelmed by the requirements of teaching both the physical act of producing letters and letter-sound associations in the two hours of teaching time available to me each day. I wondered, could there possibly be a way in which I might teach all the necessary physical writing skills and writing process at the same time?

In searching for a vehicle which could do just that, I reflected back on my experience teaching writing in the third grade. There I'd found that the most efficient way of teaching the children was to write with them, sharing the different steps of MY writing process from brainstorming for topic choice, to publication. I wondered, could this approach work with these much younger children?

It should, I reasoned. After all, we do not teach young children much of anything by mere verbal directions. We show them. Imagine teaching five-year-olds how to tie their shoes using only verbal directions. Try it. First take the string in your right hand (already you're in trouble since most five-year-olds don't know their right from their left) then cross it over the string in your left hand (trouble again) then bring it under and around through the space made by the cross. . . . It gets worse from there.

Of course we don't do this. When children have watched us tie shoes often enough, and they are sufficiently coordinated to handle fine motor tasks and sequential directions, we pull them along beside us and SHOW them how to tie: Watch me. Take one string in this hand, see? Now watch, cross it over the string in this hand, see? Now watch. Put this end under . . . etc. After many repetitions and much practice, children learn to tie, not by verbal instruction alone, but by following our model.

I decided to experiment with demonstrating the writing process for just a few months to see if it would work. If it didn't, I planned to abandon it and return to more traditional methods of teaching.

Once I had decided to model the process, I was again unsure of where to start! Since children's earliest writing usually begins with drawing, I finally chose to start there (Temple, Nathan and Burris, 1982). I thought that if I drew and then captioned pictures, it would both place the instruction at the level the children had achieved, and expose them to something they had not yet done (writing and reading). In order to communicate that pictures can have meaning and convey messages, I called my model a "story picture."

After much deliberation, I chose the overhead projector on which to present my model. The overhead produces an image which is large, clear, and easily seen. In addition, young children seem to be especially attentive to the screen when the lights are dimmed.

I had three objectives for the first session:

1. To draw a picture.
2. To tell something about that picture in order to present the concept of narrative thinking on paper.
3. To write a short caption for the picture in both inventive and conventional spelling to introduce letter recognition, letter-sound associations and the concept of inventive and conventional spelling.

It was hard for me to draw that first story picture. Just as some people are afraid to write, I am no artist and am self-conscious about my drawings. Before beginning to draw, I talked about the trip to the tide pools the class had taken the day before, and how it had given me an idea for my story picture.

The room was totally silent as I drew (Fig. 1). I remarked that I did not draw people very well, and Shannon consoled me by remarking that he "had trouble drawing people too ... even dogs."

I finished the picture and wrote the words: Yesterday I caught my first crab (Ystrda I kt mi frst krab) in inventive spelling at the top of the page, sounding out the words and writing the letters for the most

FIGURE 1

prominent sounds. I explained that this kind of writing was called inventive spelling; it was the kind children first learned. I also wrote the conventional spelling at the bottom of the page, saying that this writing was the kind most adults did and the kind the children found in print.

So the children would not be overwhelmed by too much new material, I stopped there and passed out crayons and paper for them to draw their own story pictures. As they finished, my aide and I talked briefly with the children about their pictures and wrote a short statement in conventional spelling at the bottom of each one, trying to keep as close to the children's own words as possible. We continued to work daily with the children, helping them to write about their pictures in their own inventive spelling. Our transcription of their words was printed in conventional spelling at the bottom of the page.

I continued modeling with the children in much the same way for several weeks. Gradually they began to participate: reminding me I'd forgotten to draw in a nose, offering ideas for pictures, and helping with the inventive spelling. As I'd voice a sound, /b/ for example, they'd hear a classmate say "B" and it would appear on the screen at the same time. The room always darkened, the children's attention was focused on what they were seeing and hearing. Although my drawing did not improve, my willingness to keep trying seemed to let the children know that it was OK to be imperfect, that children weren't the only ones who had a hard time making their hands do what they wanted them to.

Seeing that the children continued to maintain a high degree of interest in my story pictures, I began slowly to introduce other concepts into this modeling time. I began each modeling session with three main objectives. One was always letter-sound associations. Others fell into areas such as:

topic choice
different writing styles
different writing formats
writing before drawing
correspondence between inventive and conventional spelling
blends
punctuation
extended narration (books)
reading strategies

For example, when I wrote: "This is a mean Giant! He is mean because his teeth hurt!" I wrote in inventive spelling, demonstrating letters and letter-sound associations. I talked with the children about make-believe and real stories and also explained the use of the exclamation point.

Because this was an experimental approach, I had no prescribed curriculum to follow. I soon found, however, that careful observation of what the children were doing in their story pictures and inventive spelling led me to see what they needed to know or were ready to be exposed to.

As the children matured, they moved from drawing objects to drawing pictures showing action (Graves, 1983). The children's writing correspondingly moved from simple labelling of their pictures—"a house", "my dog"—to action phrases and sentences, "A dog eating," "I am sliding on the pond" (Hilliker, 1982). These action-filled captions continually contained words ending in -ing. Because -ing is impossible to write in inventive spelling, I decided to teach it to them. They seemed to delight in knowing something so simple. They'd grin slyly as we came across an -ing word in our writing. They knew I would ask, "And what three letters say -ing?" They knew the answer.

Later th, ch, and sh followed along with frequently used sight words like and, day, too, and the. Initially the children confused the blends and used them interchangeably in their writing. With repetition, however, they slowly began to sort them out.

Although I primarily modeled writing, I also taught the children different reading strategies. I consistently compared inventive and conventional spelling, noting likenesses and differences between the two. Sometimes I would draw and write without telling them what I had written, and ask them to guess what I'd written from the picture or any words they might know. Often I'd leave out a word and ask them to guess what it would be, using the context of the other words and clues from the picture (Durkin, 1978).

When over half the class was writing with little help, I felt it was time to introduce longer narrative. I changed my model from the writing of individual story pictures to the writing of books. My books continued to consist of pictures with inventive and conventional spellings top and bottom, but they became a series of pictures which told a story or adhered to one particular theme. I wrote a page or two in my overhead projector book each day.

When I had completed my first book, I brought out extra paper and a stapler, and waited anxiously to see if any children would follow my example. Most of them hastened to staple pages (and pages) together. Interestingly, those who were capable of writing longer pieces did just that. Those who were not simply made each page in their books a separate story picture, which did not relate either to their book title or to the other pages in the book.

I was very disappointed that Jason, one of my most able writers, did not immediately start writing a book. This disappointment was short-lived. Three days after we began writing books, he brought me a story picture at the end of writing time. The picture showed a cutaway view of Jason's house with him sitting by the television, writing (Fig. 2). At the top of his picture he had written: I MAd A BuK i FiN NiThT IT uoN SAbrbAy (I made a book I finished it on Saturday). At my request he brought the book in to share the following day. It was a detailed account of a day in his mother's life, which included a trip to the beach where she surfed on giant waves.

During the daily demonstration sessions I began to notice that some of the children were getting quite good at translating both the inventive and conventional spellings on the screen. However, when first Andrew, and then Meg, told me that they could read, I'm afraid I really didn't take them seriously. However, after Jason, and then Maura and Roger, confided in me, "I can read now!" I began to listen. Could they have somehow learned to read while I wasn't looking?

Paying closer attention, I could see that these children were indeed reading. They could read filmstrip headings, library book titles, early reader books, job lists, and their own writing. Andrew eventually took it

FIGURE 2

upon himself to read all the take-home notices to the children at his table.

I was amazed. I never really anticipated that these kindergarten children would learn to read without traditional teaching methods. Certainly we'd been learning how to write, but we'd had no reading books, no groups, no workbooks, no flashcards. No course work or background reading had prepared me for this. As the year progressed and child after child, one third in all, spontaneously started reading, I had to admit that somehow the combination of their own writing and watching the writing and reading process go on day after day, must have somehow provided them access to the print around them.

Despite apparent success, practicing something so experimental left me with several concerns. One of my most serious concerns about using demonstrations with the children every day was that they would copy what I was doing and not expand within their own work. To guard against this, I intentionally spent a few minutes at the start of each writing period explaining what I would write about and why.

I wrote about feelings: "I am crabby today because I have a headache," explaining that writing about my bad feelings made me feel better; and that writers often write about their feelings. I wrote make-believe stories: "Once upon a time there was a dragon who lived in a blue cave. He lit charcoal grills for a living," telling them I found it fun to make up stories about imaginary things. I also wrote factual things: "It is getting warmer because the earth is tipping toward the sun," which reflected classroom study. I stressed by example that writing was a personal activity and differed with each person's needs.

I can thankfully say it must have worked. Few of the children directly copied my topic of the day, and those who did copy my topic choices did so for only a short time. I did find the children were fond of copying each other's topics! One rainbow book led to ten. A He-Man adventure picture led to six more. However, the children also drew and wrote about other things: trees cracking in lightning, dinosaurs having parties, snow storms, sledding expeditions, parent-child trips, and younger sisters waking up too early. They also produced a retelling of "The Return of the Jedi," "The Snow Queen," and "Cinderella." A glance through the children's work made it clear that they were writing from their own life experience, interest, and perspective.

A second concern was that, with such a strong emphasis on my story picture format, the children would not expand their writing and reading efforts beyond the model. By mid-year, however, these fears were allayed. Children began to ask, "What does this say?" about print other than that which I was producing. They began writing down each other's names and phone numbers. Often they brought in writing or attempted writing from home. At midyear parent conferences, many parents reported that their children were constantly drawing, writing, and trying to read at home.

A third concern, of course, was whether or not the children in my classes were learning the basic skills expected of them: alphabet recognition and letter-sound associations. It was not enough to have one third of the children reading and writing. The other two thirds had to show skill acquisition. By the end of the year, all but five of my forty-six students could randomly recognize all upper and lower case letters. Letter-sound associations were also strong in all but a few. Most children had picked up *-ing, the, day* and *too*. They had learned all that was required and more than I'd expected.

Perhaps, somehow, showing how it is done brings children into the writing and reading processes. By participating in the adult's processes as they learn how themselves, children come to see writing and reading as something over which they can have some control. They see writing and reading as they occur, not as the product of some mysterious activity of which a person is only capable after several years of school.

It isn't a mystery. You can do it too. Come here, I'll show you. Watch me!

References   Bissex, Glenda. *GNYS AT WRK: A Child Learns to Write and Read.* Cambridge: Harvard University Press, 1980.

Durkin, Delores. *Teaching Them to Read.* Boston: Allyn and Bacon, 1978.

Graves, Donald H. *Writing: Teachers and Children at Work.* Exeter, N.H.: Heinemann Educational Books, 1983.

Hilliker, Judith. "Labelling to Beginning Narrative: Four Kindergarten Children Learn to Write." In *Understanding Writing: Ways of Observing, Learning and Teaching K–8,* ed. T. Newkirk and N. Atwell. Urbana, Illinois: National Council of Teachers of English, 1982.

Temple, Charles A., Nathan, Ruth, and Burris, Nancy. *The Beginnings of Writing.* Boston: Allyn and Bacon, 1982.

A Teacher Talks to Parents

WINNIFRED BRAUN

The January chill began to creep beneath the door of my grade one classroom. A trickle of questions came from parents, followed by an icy cascade of questions about what the children were doing and why. At first it felt as if all the parents were discontented, but as the weeks unfolded I realized that these parents were in a minority. Still, something had to be done as news of community coffee meetings among grade one parents began to filter into school. Dissatisfied parents were attempting to persuade the majority to join their side.

I was convinced that the children were progressing. It was clear to me that they were gaining an awareness of the reading and writing processes. They moved freely, but with purpose, choosing materials for the next book they wanted to write, discussing their next writing topic with a friend, or reading a book to a partner. I was happy with the strategies the children were learning to use when reading and writing. I wanted to show the parents that their children were learning to read and write, and enjoying it.

Our school has an open-door policy. Parents are free to come into our classrooms to help or observe. Some parents come regularly, some come once or twice, some not at all. This can be more threatening than I used to think, because the parents who come rarely, see only an isolated part of the program. I later saw this as the breeding ground for the questions: "Why don't you use a set of readers in the classroom?" "Why aren't all the stories written to completion?" and on and on. The parents were, in essence, asking why I wasn't teaching their children to read and write the way they had been taught.

By February, pressure from parents seemed too great to withstand. I felt tired and discouraged. The children had well-established language backgrounds and were ready to leap ahead in their learning, but I used my energy to respond to parents instead of teach. I became convinced some children heard their parents' concerns at home, for occasionally they said, "I don't want to do this" or "This is boring." Such remarks were a new experience for me and didn't help my diminishing confidence. After several meetings with my principal, we decided to hold a parents' meeting.

We had scheduled meetings in the fall to explain programs and philosophies, but now I realized that in September parents only saw the beginning of the program and may have found it difficult to see how it fit together. I hadn't known for sure myself in September, since this was my first year teaching grade one. I became more convinced I was on the right track, however, as I reviewed my program for the parents' night.

Armed with index cards of my main points, an extended version typed on crisp, white paper (just in case I forgot what the points meant because of nervousness), and a pile of transparencies, I was ready. I still felt a chill among some of the parents, but the coldness mingled with the warmth of colleagues and the majority of parents who had come to give support.

First, I took the parents back to the beginning of the year. I told them about the eager faces expecting to read, expecting a magic wand to grant their wish. I had no illusions and no magic wand. A few children knew how to read and most knew that a story exists between the covers of a book. I had listened to the children relate their experiences, read with them, and we had talked about stories. I had learned that many of the children came equipped with rich oral language and background experiences.

The parents laughed when I showed a poem written in Chinese (Figure 1) and asked them to read it. The ice began to break. I had their attention and my nervousness faded. I explained that at the beginning of the year, many of the children were bewildered by all the words they saw. Like the parents looking at the Chinese characters,

FIGURE 1

低頭思故鄉
舉頭望明月
疑是地上霜
牀前明月光
夜思

李白

some children weren't sure whether to read from right to left or from top to bottom. Their confusion was natural. Had I pushed the children into learning isolated parts of reading, without a firm understanding of how the whole system worked, the children would have become more confused and lost interest.

Since I wanted to extend the children's knowledge of reading and writing from what they already knew, I explained how literature was central to my program. The children and I spent many hours reading nursery rhymes, poems, and stories, often until they were memorized. Memorization, I pointed out, helped the children learn what it feels like to be a good reader—that is, to be a fluent reader. Familiar materials helped the children evolve as readers, and new materials expanded their repertoire.

I walked the parents through a poem, "I saw, I saw" (Figure 2), to show how I helped the children extend their knowledge of the reading process. I wasn't primarily interested in how many words I taught the children to read. Rather, I wanted to help them develop strategies to become fluent readers. I explained that the children and I read through the poem (Version A) together. Then we covered up Version A and worked through Version B. Since the children knew about the zoo they had no trouble making sense of a sentence like "I saw, I saw, I saw / A _____ at the zoo." They knew that "A" was a signal for a noun (in this case an animal, since we were talking about the zoo). The parents saw how the children used meaning and word order as signals, something they did when they talked before they came to school.

I continued to explain that my program didn't include a menu of isolated sounds, letters, and rules. Instead, I wanted the children to

---

FIGURE 2

I saw, I saw, I saw	I __aw, I __aw, I __aw
A lion at the zoo.	A __ion at the __oo.
I saw, I saw, I saw	I __aw, I __aw, I __aw
A baby tiger, too.	A __aby __iger, too.
I saw, I saw, I saw	I __aw, I __aw, I __aw
A great big kangaroo.	A __ __eat __ig __angaroo.
I saw, I saw, I saw	I __aw, I __aw, I __aw
I saw them at the zoo.	I __aw __ __em at the __oo.
(A)	**(B)**

find out how written language works. However, I didn't want to leave the parents with the impression that I neglected phonics, as some assumed in January, so I showed how I introduced sound/letter elements. In the example above, I had asked the children, "What letter do I need to begin lion? Listen to yourself say the word *lion*. Do you know someone whose name starts with the same sound as *lion*?" The children and I worked through the poem together. We listened, we made predictions, we checked our predictions and reread. There was no risk and no failure.

My use of literature instead of a basal series concerned the parents, so I presented some of my reasons. I explained that I wanted to show the children what was in store for them as readers and writers. Long before Christmas break, they learned that an important part of reading was to enjoy it. I don't want my students to grow up to echo some parents who have told me they don't read because they never learned to like it. I want to help build a foundation for their future.

Literature expanded the children's background experiences and extended their vocabularies. I told parents how stories he had heard beforehand allowed Stephen to include more detail and a richer vocabulary in his own story about an owl, and how Hena would not have written her tale of the groundhog's lost shadow had she not heard related stories and discussed them. I told the parents about the day Jamie decided to write about flowers and went to the library to find books to help her. She already knew how to extend her knowledge.

What fascinated me, and began to fascinate the parents, was the unconscious use of book language or the language of authors some children used in their own writing. Greg's story (Figure 3) was original but the list of characters was similar to the book *One Monday Morning*. He had internalized some of the structure. Greg's story helped the parents understand another reason for using literature in my classroom.

The parents had also expressed concern about writing. I knew the children were enthusiastic about their writing, and I wanted the parents to understand that writing, when allowed to develop like speech, does not start from little pieces and gradually build up. It begins with ideas; the children write down their ideas, and then share them through publishing. The excitement that comes with the accomplishment motivates children to write more. Like speech, the refinements evolve as the children learn to communicate with an audience.

The children wanted others to read their pieces of writing, so they discovered the importance of moving from invented spellings to conventional spellings. It wasn't an easy process, I told the parents, but the children learned a great deal about conventional spelling by using invented spelling and by looking at more and more print (Figures 4, 5

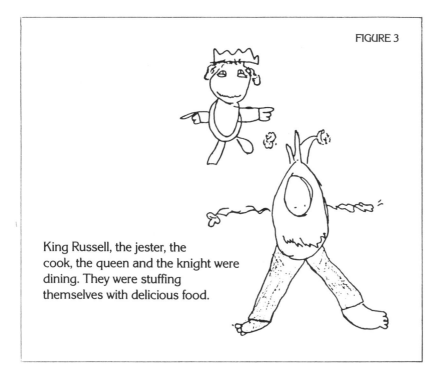

King Russell, the jester, the cook, the queen and the knight were dining. They were stuffing themselves with delicious food.

FIGURE 3

and 6). Had I stressed spelling and mechanics, I wouldn't have observed the same high quality of ideas. I went on to say that in a conference setting the children and I decided which pieces would be published for the class library and these were edited.

The children wrote with a sense of responsibility because they wrote for themselves and for each other. There was sharing, talking, and reading, which helped the children explore the purposes and pleasures of writing.

As the meeting closed, the parents had a better understanding of my child-centered language program. They knew that literature was central to the program, that phonics was taught (but not as they had been taught), and that the children were learning about language through reading and writing. The puzzle was by no means complete, but the parents left seeing many pieces in place, and as their children continued to learn, more pieces would fall into place.

My program had weaknesses, certainly, but the parents' meeting allowed me to focus on the strengths. The parents' support came in the weeks and months that followed. One mother wrote: "Last time I read *The Hungry Thing* to Jessy. This time she read it to me."

This episode of Greg's story demonstrates his use of invented spelling. What is important here is that he is learning to tell a story on paper. He is combining the resources available to him – pictures, invented spellings and the odd conventional spelling. It all makes sense to Greg.

Parents were satisfied that benchmarks of learning bound in primer or workbook covers could be replaced with interesting (not always tidy) pieces of writing. They saw enthusiasm about reading and writing as a significant indication of learning.

My communication with parents provided a valuable learning experience—for them, and also for me. I learned the importance of explaining to parents what I do in school and the importance of justifying my program, particularly those aspects which are foreign to parents' own school experiences. The effort I put forth in explanation has been valuable for my own professional growth.

FIGURE 5

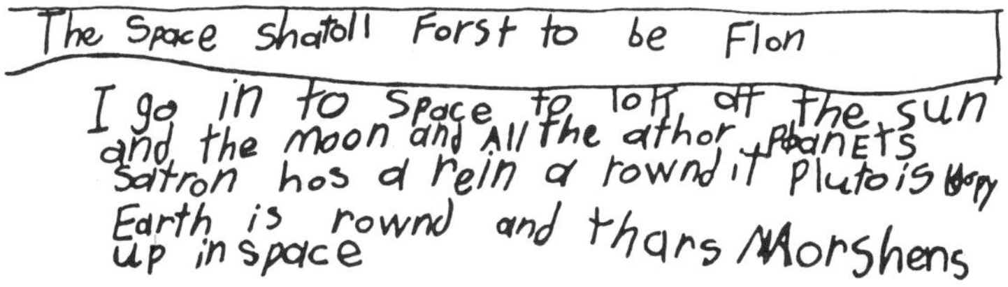

> The Space shatoll Forst to be Flon
>
> I go in to Space to lok at the sun
> and the moon and All the athor planets
> Satron hos a rein a rownd it Pluto is tiny
> Earth is rownd and thars Morshens
> up in space

Stephen has already progressed to the point where he uses more conventional spellings than his own inventions. As in the case of Greg, to constrain Stephen to communicate only what he can spell would impede his flow of ideas, his enthusiasm for writing and his confidence as a writer.

FIGURE 6

The next day I was
eating my breakfast with
my Granny and Grandpop.
for lunch we aet soap all
for dinner we aet carrots and
cucumber and tomatoes

Till recently Tanya used many invented spellings. She has found that as she uses more and more conventional spellings others find it easier to read her stories. This is important to her. In other words, Tanya has a good reason for consciously using conventional spellings.

Yes, the ending to the cold winter saga is a happy one. My efforts have not gone unrewarded. This is a new September, and I am now a grade two teacher. I see the familiar faces of many young readers and writers who are with me at their parents' request.

References   Shulevitz, Uri. *One Monday Morning.* New York: Charles Scribner's Sons, 1967.

Slepian, Jan and Ann Seidler. *The Hungry Thing.* New York: Scholastic Book Services, 1967.

Reading: A Monitor for Writing

HEATHER HEMMING

Geoffrey is a first-grade author who wants his audience to like the sound of his writing. So, he monitors his writing by reading. He consciously revises his text by switching back and forth between the role of reader and writer. Because I was interested in this aspect of Geoffrey's writing process, I questioned him about the role reading played in his revision of *The Day I Auditioned* (Figure 1).

How do you decide which words to cross out?
GEOFFREY: *You mean how do I know?*
Yes.
GEOFFREY: *I read it over. . . . Hey that doesn't sound good. I should change it. Here it said, "thing." I didn't want it. It said, "They wanted me to do this thing!" I didn't need "thing." "They asked me to do this," sounds good! I didn't make a spaceship either. I just pretended.*
How did you decide to make the changes?
GEOFFREY: *I didn't want it there. It just didn't sound good! I didn't need it.*
What about the part you added?
GEOFFREY: *Like . . . because you . . . I wanted to put it here (points to the middle of the page). If I started about the other people then that meant I left this out (points to the added section marked with an asterisk).*
Why is that important?
GEOFFREY: *It's important because it is part of the story. It's sort of . . . if I didn't tell the people, it wouldn't sound good and they wouldn't know that part.*

When I stop and think about this conference with Geoffrey, I know not only that he is aware of his shifting back and forth between the roles of reader and writer, but also that he knows why this kind of switch is necessary. His words need to "sound good" to be part of the voice he wants in his writing. When I thought about his behavior and his comments, I wondered how his writing environment fostered this awareness. First I tried to identify key factors, but the more I thought about it, the clearer it became. There was only one factor. My mind always came back to *time!*

FIGURE 1

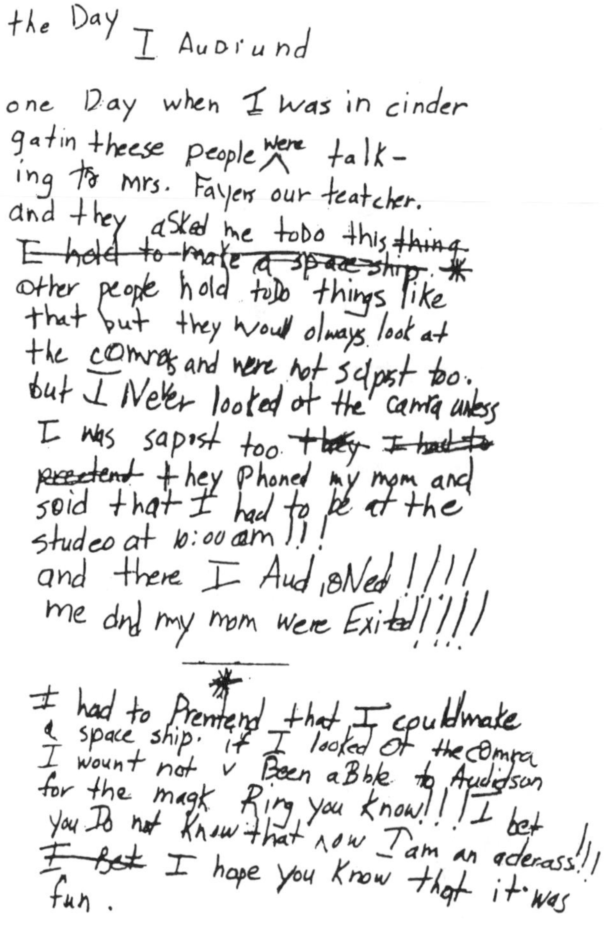

the Day I Audiund

one Day when I was in cinder
gatin theese people were talking to mrs. Fayers our teatcher.
and they asked me tobo this thing.
~~I hold to make a space ship.~~ *
other people hold tobo things like
that but they woud olways look at
the comras and were not sapst too.
but I Never looked ot the camra unless
I was sapost too. ~~they I had to~~
~~precetend~~ they Phoned my mom and
soid that I had to be at the
studeo at 10:00 am !!!
and there I Aud,oNed !!//
me dnd my mom were Exited!!//

I had to Premtend that I couldmake
a space ship. if I looked ot the comra
I wount not v Been aBble to Auddsan
for the magk Ring you know!!! I bet
you Do not know that now I am an aderass!!!
~~I Bet~~ I hope you know that it was
fun .

The Day I Auditioned   *Translation*

One day when I was in Kindergarten these people were talking to Mrs. Fayers our teacher. And they asked me to do this. I had to pretend that I could make a space ship. If I looked at the camera I would not have been able to audition for the Magic Ring you know!!! I bet you do not know now I am an actress!!! I hope you know it was fun. Other people had to do things like that but they would always look at the camera and they were not suppose to. But I never looked at the camera unless I was suppose to. They phoned my mom and said that I had to be at the studio at 10:00 a.m.!!! And there I auditioned!!!!! Me and my mom were excited!!!!!

Teachers are always conscious of time, a precious commodity in all classrooms. Like businessmen, we often think in terms of payoff. Can I afford to spend time on this activity? What will the profits be for my students? Lucille Kroeker as the first grade teacher and myself as resource person will testify that our first grade writing program did take time—blocks of time during which we did not hurry the children. We encouraged them to make discoveries about the writing process. We felt the time was well-spent because we wanted our young authors to make just such discoveries as Geoffrey's about the monitoring role reading plays in writing. We considered Murray's (1982) statement: "the act of reading is inseparable from the act of writing," and we provided time to nurture in the children an awareness of a role reading plays in writing.

I encouraged the children to spend time "playing around" when they composed. They engaged in self-directed writing activities during several periods each week. If they wished to spend time creating a writing plan, revising, reading and rereading their stories, or thinking about their writing, I encouraged them to do so. I provided time for them to formulate ideas about how the process of writing works for them, and I believe this is valuable time, because students generate their own ideas. For example, Geoffrey had time to play around with the "sound" of his story, *The Day I Auditioned.* He used exclamation marks, "Me and my mom were excited!!!" and talked to his reader, "I bet you do not know that now I am an actress." He revised his story by thinking about how he could make it "sound good" for his audience.

Time to Play with Language

My conviction that students need time is reinforced when I compare how Geoffrey composes with how some of the fifth or sixth grade students I worked with a couple of years ago composed. I still remember wondering why these students did not read when they wrote. Their writing seemed to lack a sense of control, and they frequently reached dead ends when the words stopped coming. Now when I stop and think about it, I realize that it is no wonder these authors struggled with their writing. They barely had time to come up with a topic before I demanded a copy of their story. Time for them to think about how language works was neither discussed nor encouraged. My concern was that their stories be on my desk at the end of a thirty-minute period.

The objectives of our writing program were based on research in metacognition. Metacognition is an individual's knowledge of his own cognitive processes (Flavell, 1976). Vygotsky (1962) suggests that there are two distinct phases in the development of knowledge: 1) its automatic unconscious acquisition, followed by 2) gradual increases in ac-

Time to Question Their Own Process

tive control over knowledge. This distinction captures the separation between knowledge and metacognitive understanding (Brown, 1980).

Gates (1983) suggests that executive readers function at a meta-cognitive level, when they know and deliberately orchestrate their comprehension efforts. I wanted to encourage our young writers to become aware of the strategies they could use in their writing at a metacognitive level. I felt that writers who had a conscious understanding of and control over their composing would become executive writers.

Brown (1980) and Gates (1983) maintain that, because executive readers monitor their own reading, they know when they are off target. They know when there is a problem and they know why. I felt that if writers could become aware of the factors that affected their composing, such as the monitoring role of reading, then they could move toward a position of control over their writing. To encourage metacognitive awareness we held individual conferences with the students. During these times we talked about both the content of their stories and the process they used when they wrote.

For example, Kelly initiated the following conference with me. She wanted to discuss her efforts to elaborate parts of her story, *My Silver Ring* (Figure 2). In addition, the conference provided her with a chance to explore her use of reading as part of her writing.

KELLY: *I added something to my story I want you to hear.*
  How do you do that?
KELLY: *I added something.*
  Is that all you have to do?
KELLY: *Go back over ... to see if it's all right to do it.*
  How do you go back over it?
KELLY: *Read it.*
  Why do you go back over and read it?
KELLY: *We need to read it to see if we can add more. Make it more interesting for the people who want to read it.*

Kelly realizes that she reads to monitor her writing and deliberately plans how she will elaborate so that others will find her story interesting. When she responds to the question, "Why do you go back over it and read?" her answer begins, "We need to read. ..." Her use of "we" seems to signify that she had generalized her understanding of the use of reading to monitor her composing. She knows that it too is a part of the writing process of others.

My role as audience allowed me to question Kelly about how she actually made changes in her story and encouraged her to think about the role reading plays in her composing. Calkins (1983) points out that the presence of a listener encourages writers to become readers of their own texts. Similarly, the presence of an audience who

FIGURE 2

I like My Yeng
beciqse it is selvr
Rabbingt reng

This is where she
began to add to her
story.

I get it fram My mom
and
My
DaD. and
I get Fram Sarg
and I like it clos
To

I war it
il The tiem

My Silver Ring   *Translation*

I like my ring because it is a silver rabbit ring. I got it from my
mom and my dad. And I got it from Santa Claus too. And I like it. I
wear it all the time.

can question the readers about what they do when they compose, encourages writers to think about what is involved in the act of writing.
My questions about the process helped provide Kelly with a framework within which to examine her ideas about the role reading played
in her writing. The sequential nature of the questions encouraged her
to express why she used reading in her writing. Such questioning encourages children to explore on their own.

I take full advantage of the discoveries young authors can make when
I set aside class time for them to share with each other. At the end of
each writing period, students read their stories and discuss their com-

Time to Question
Each Others'
Processes

posing with one another. When I am aware of a student's specific discovery about the writing process, I use it to focus a group conference so others may share in the learning.

During an individual conference, Melanie spoke about the role reading played when she revised *The Crystal Ball*. During this conference (which follows), I realized how valuable her insights could be for other writers in the class.

Why did you decide to cross out those words?
MELANIE: *I wanted it to make sense.*
How do you go about making those kinds of changes?
MELANIE: *Well ... Umm. I read it over and this (points to "saw a wich") wasn't important, so I crossed it out.*
Then what did you do?
MELANIE: *I just added!*

FIGURE 3

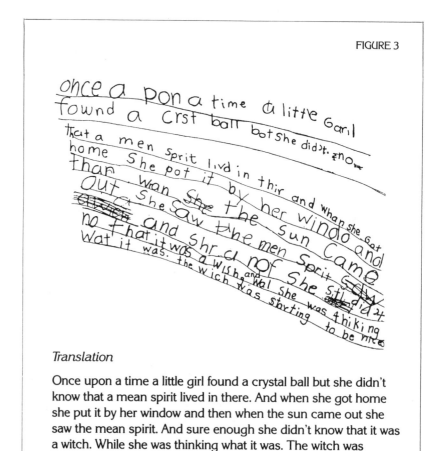

Translation

Once upon a time a little girl found a crystal ball but she didn't know that a mean spirit lived in there. And when she got home she put it by her window and then when the sun came out she saw the mean spirit. And sure enough she didn't know that it was a witch. While she was thinking what it was. The witch was starting to be nice.

Melanie's understanding of the monitoring role reading plays in her writing functions at a metacognitive level. She is aware that she deliberately used reading as a part of her writing to orchestrate her composing. She felt that "saw a wich" detracted from the sense of her story and she knew exactly how to alleviate the problem these words created: she omitted them.

I told the other children that Melanie and I had talked about her writing and we wanted to share something with them. Then Melanie and I went through our dialogue again, but this time before the class. There are some students in the class, such as Geoffrey and Kelly, who can see Melanie's experience in relation to their own writing. But others find it harder because they are either not at a point where they use reading as a part of their writing, or they use it at an unconscious level. I hoped that some of the information from the discussion with Melanie would act as a spark to these children and their learning. I told the students I wanted them in the future to think about how and why they make changes in their writing so that they would go back to their seats with unanswered questions about the role reading plays in their writing. Thinking about these questions could provide a focus for future exploration in their own writing.

Writers who use reading to monitor their composing gain real control over it. In my classroom, I want to hear my students comment: "When I read this over I don't like the way it sounds for the people who are going to read it. I want to change it." I want them to realize that authors who consciously read to monitor their writing, write words their readers want to hear.

References

Brown, Ann L. "Metacognitive Development and Reading." In *Theoretical Issues in Reading Comprehension,* ed. Rand J. Spiro, Bertram C. Bruce, and William F. Brewer. Hillsdale, N. J.: Lawrence Erlbaum, 1980.

Calkins, Lucy McCormick. *Lessons From a Child:* Exeter, N. H.: Heinemann Educational Books, 1983.

Flavell, John H. "Metacognitive Aspects of Problem Solving." In *The Nature of Intelligence,* ed. L. B. Resnick. Hillsdale, N. J.: Lawrence Earlbaum, 1976.

Gates, Dale D. "Turning Polite Guests into Executive Readers." *Language Arts* 60 (1983):977–82.

Giacobbe, Mary Ellen. "A Writer Reads, A Reader Writes." In *Understanding Writing,* ed. by Thomas Newkirk and Nancie Atwell. Chelmsford, MA.: NEREX, Inc., 1982: 114–125.

Murray, Donald M. "Teaching the Other Self: The Writer's First Reader." In *Learning by Teaching,* Montclair, N. J.: Boynton/Cook, 1982.

Vygotsky, L. S. *Thought and Language,* Cambridge: MIT Press, 1962.

PART
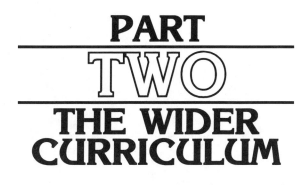
TWO
THE WIDER
CURRICULUM

Beyond the
Writing Table

KATHY MATTHEWS

Writing across the curriculum isn't as formidable as it sounds. Children need not wait until third or fourth grade to begin, nor must they only write *about* specific curricular topics. Writing across the curriculum is simply a matter of extending the writing process beyond the writing table, and applying the principles and opportunities of the process to a variety of thinking situations. Like the six- and seven-year-olds in my past pre-first and first grade classes who have successfully integrated writing into their daily activities, even the youngest writers can come to view writing not merely as a personal narrative in a booklet or journal, but as the natural complement to everything they do.

I do three things in my classroom to extend writing across the curriculum:

1. Develop an accepting environment
2. Ask questions
3. Provide a wide range of writing experiences

First, and most important of all, the children and I work together to create a climate of trust and acceptance. When one's feelings and ideas are respected and not ridiculed it becomes easier to take risks, to share oneself with others, and to be able to stand firm about one's thinking or writing in the face of questions and comments.

This means, of course, that as a teacher I must be willing to accept information and logic that, by most standards, are inaccurate. Just as I view invented spelling as a developmental process that does not diminish the quality of the content of a written piece, so too, I emphasize the fact *that* a child writes and thinks, not whether the content of the writing or thinking is accurate or infallible. It is far more important that Jon chose to speculate in writing about the changes in his jar of three green beans than that he justified the liquid in the bottom of the jar as "water 'cause it was cold and snow (mold) got on the beans and now it's spring and it's warmer and the snow's meltin'."

At this young age, speculation and logic—particularly in science—are governed by characteristics inherent in children's cognitive development. Their logic is intuitive and ruled, for the most part, by perception and convenience. As a science experience, for example, the children made cardboard thaumotropes with a picture of a tiger on one side and a cage on the other. When they spun them like an old-fashioned button toy, the tiger appears to be in the cage. Asked how this could be, the children typically wrote:

AT LSK LAK A TIGR AN A KG KS WN YOY SPN AT LSKC LAK THE CATS MUVA. *(It looks like a tiger in a cage 'cause when you spin it looks like the cat's movin'.)*

BRPRLE ET SI MREG AND THE TOIKV IS MARK. *(Probably it's magic and the tiger is magic.)*

BCUS THE LIS ON THE TIRE AND IT LOOKS LIK THE TIGRE IS IN THE KAJE. *(Because there's lines on the tiger and it looks like the tiger's in the cage.)*

THE KRDBORD IS TO FAST FOR THE HUMIN IS TO CE. *(The cardboard is too fast for the human eyes to see.)*

In an accepting environment, statements like these inevitably lead to discussion in which the children gently challenge each other, read and voice their own hypotheses, and often, are stimulated to read and write about the phenomena on their own.

The second thing I do is to surround the children with questions to encourage them to think. The questions are open-ended because I want them to think for themselves and for the sake of the process of thinking, not because I expect them to arrive at any preconceived answers. The child who is accustomed to encountering questions like, "How are these two the same?" during an experience in art or science can more successfully respond to the question, "How do these two parts of your story go together?" during a writing conference.

I usually write a morning message to the children and conclude it with a question to which I encourage them to respond, e.g., "Yesterday when I looked in the onion bag I found this onion with green shoots growing out of the top. How can it grow without dirt?" The children respond if they choose, and at a later time in the day, they share these responses with the rest of the class. For this particular question the responses:

PRABLEE THER WAD A LITL DDT. *(Probably there was a little dirt.)*

MAB THE ONION DAT GOR RIT. *(Maybe the onion didn't grow right.)*

yielded interesting discussion not only about the nature or truth of each speculation but about the children's thinking and writing processes as well.

Often I post questions in different classroom areas as a stimulus for a specific activity. A child at the science table, for example, might encounter a styrofoam cup, a deflated balloon, and the question: "How can you lift the cup with the balloon?" Someone at the art table might be asked: "What can you make that you would find in the woods?" whereas another child visiting the classroom animals might respond to the question: "How are the rabbit and the guinea pig the same?" The children read the questions, experiment or create as the task requires, and then write about their experience:

I PT THE BL UDR THE CAP AD BLAT. IT WAT UP UND THE BKAS THE AR AS SDAK. *(I put the balloon under the cup and blew it. It went up under the [side] because the air is strong.)*

WE GAV THAM VCHTABLS. *(We give them vegetables.)*

Sometimes I mimeograph a question for the entire group to respond to at once. We then take turns reading, explaining, justifying, and discussing individual speculations. To the question: "What did you discover about the rocks?" individual children responded:

WTE THE MECE YOU CUN BRAK ONE BES AND IT WILL CEM OUT WTE TO. *(With the mica you can break one piece and it will come out white, too.)*

WN YOU LL THE KERDL AE LL LRE. *(When you look [through] the crystal it looks blurry.)*

I FOAT OT FAT THE REK GODT HV LITLE PVTR AV MIK. *(I found out that rocks could have little pieces of mica.)*

The third thing I do is to surround the children with opportunities to write. The journals and booklets which house their personal narratives are vital to the heart and soul of our reading/writing program, but there are chances to write in other ways as well. One important source of writing is our class newspaper. Each morning, as part of our group meeting, I solicit news from the class leader that I then print on large chart paper (this initial item also serves the dual purpose of allowing me to conduct a short skills lesson). The paper is then available for the children to record their personal news until the "deadline," when the reporters read their respective items to the class.

The children intuitively differentiate news writing from narrative and modify their style to reflect the difference. They report on the weather:

IT RAND TODAY. WE KDNT GO OTSD. *(It rained today. We couldn't go outside.)*

on sport events:

WE PLD SKR AT RESS. WE WN THE ATHR TEEM 10 TO 0. *(We played soccer at recess. We won the other team 10 to 0.)*

interesting phenomena:

I SAW A MAN DRIVEN BAKWORDS ON THE STRET. *(I saw a man driving backwards on the street.)*

personal events:

IT IS MY DOGIS BRTHDAY PRETE SON. *(It is my dog's birthday pretty soon.)*

I LT A TOOTH. *(I lost a tooth.)*

I WTA TO THE AIA DKTR HE SDI MI AIAS WR BTTA. *(I went to the eye doctor. He said my eyes were better.)*

personal tragedies:

LST NIT I KRID BKAS MY GRANFARHR DID. *(Last night I cried because my grandfather died.)*

and special moments:

LAS NIT MY MOM R M IN THE RKR. *(Last night my mom rocked me in the rocker.)*

The children report about the experiences in their lives which have meaning but do not, for one reason or another, warrant the time and energy of a sequenced narrative. Indeed, news writing has a more immediate impact and can reach others in ways narratives can not. It served as an outlet for Mollie's grief, for example, as over several days she reported about her kitten's serious injuries and eventual death. The children could read her news and respond in a way she needed. Had she written a narrative, her need for empathy and solace might have been lost to the process of telling the story at length and from a distance.

The primary means by which I extend writing across the curriculum is by using writing books whose shape and function distinguish them from the children's narrative journals. There are books specific to activities or experiences. In the listening area, for example, the children might find a book in which they respond to a particular story tape. Perhaps there are specific questions to answer or simply space to write a review or tell about a particular part they enjoyed, as Julie did for William Steig's *Doctor Desoto:*

I LOK WN THE MOS TRC THE FKC. *(I liked when the mouse tricked the fox.)*

There are individual "area" books in which the children record their personal experiences in our activity-centered room. The entries are as diverse as the children themselves. Some write about math experiences:

I MAD A PADN. IT WAS GREEN RED GREEN RED GREEN RED. *(I made a pattern. It was green, red, green, red, green, red.)*

some about art:

TAS IS A PIG WIAKG N ITS BRN. THE SAN IS CINAKA AN HM AND BRDS FLIAK AN THE SKI. *(This is a pig walking [in front of] his barn. The sun is shining on him and birds are flying in the sky.)*

They describe how to complete an activity:

I MAD A BATRFLI WITH GOBORS. FIRST I TOK A BLUE ALASTEK AND MAD IT NTO A WING AND I DID THE SAME THEING WTH THE RED ALASTAK AND THN I PT ANTHR ALASTIK IN THE MITLL. *(I made a butterfly with geoboards. First I took a blue elastic and made it into a wing and then I did the same thing with the red elastic and then I put another elastic in the middle.)*

They record observations and discoveries:

I STANDID ON THE SKAL AND I WAD 100 PNDS. *(I standed on the scale and I weighed 100 lbs.).*

They write about feelings:

I FEL GOD ABAOT THAT I MAD A SDAR. THT IS THE THAG I FEL GOD ABAOT. (I feel good about that I made a star. That is the thing that I feel good about.)

There are also "community journals" which are kept in particular curricula areas so that children working at the area may contribute to the book if they wish. The titles reflect the specific emphasis of each: In "Smokey and Rockwell" the children write observations about our resident guinea pig and rabbit. They write about science discoveries in "Exploring," art projects in "Things We Made," plays and puppet shows in "Pretending," and environmental observations in "Outside Our Window." The lovely quality of these journals is that the children build upon each other's work. Someone writes that a cat has appeared at the birdfeeders, another adds that a squirrel is responsible for the disappearing suet bags. One child writes about the paper bag puppet she has completed, and a friend reads the description and then creates her own puppet, which she then writes about. The journals provide a wonderful cycle of writing and reading, writing and reading.

Last of all, we have special books that the children call their "End-of-the-Day" books—hardbound volumes in which the children record, then share significant events, feelings, and thoughts at the end of each day. They write about experiences with each other:

I PLAY A GAM WEF JNAFER A COMETRAHNA GAM WE ARE PLAEN ON THE ROGG JNAFER WONN. *(I played a game with Jennifer, a concentration game. We are playing on the rug. Jennifer won.)*

They write about surprises and discoveries:

IT WAS FANE WN ME SAK TRN BLLO WACH THEA SAL R. *(It was funny when my socks turned blue which they still are.)*

They write about classroom jobs they like to perform and activities they especially enjoy:

I LIKE WAN ALL THE CHDREN WR MACING THE SOWFAKS EN THE ART AREA TODAY. *(I like when all the children were making the snowflakes in the art area today.)*

I LIKE WN WE MAD A DAM WATH THE WATR GOING DON THE JAT SREM. THE JAT SREM IS A SAM WATR LILL SAMS KMIN TO THEN. *(I like when we made a dam with the water going down the jet stream. The jet stream is a stream with little streams coming into it.)*

They frequently write about feelings. Feelings of pleasure:

I LK THT WE KM BK TO SKOOL TODAY. *(I like that we came back to school today.)*

anger:

I DDNT LK ERIN LFT MY THE BK FL ON MI. *(I didn't like when Erin laughed at me when the book fell on me.)*

and of difficult lessons like learning to lose:

I DT LK KRIS BT ME T IT TO BT WE HD FN. *(I didn't like when Kris beat me two times but we had fun.)*

Often the children write about writing and the pride they feel as authors:

I LT ELRCDN M FC B. *(I like illustrating my first book.)*

I LIKE WN I PABLES MY FRD BOOK. *(I like when I published my first book.)*

   The result of providing the children with diverse opportunities, questions, and an accepting environment is that they spontaneously initiate their own writing/reading experiences and extend writing beyond even my expectations. They write about themselves and how they've changed:

HOW I'VE CHEANGED:
1. I'M BIG'R
2. I HAVE LAGR HARE *(longer hair)*
3. I HAVE BIG'R CLOTHS
4. I HAVE NEW FRANDS
5. I CAN MAC BATR THEINGS *(better things)*

They write about art activities:

I MADE A ULNASA OUT IV YARN. I RAPT THE YARN AROND CARDBORD TAIN I TID IT AND IT TORND OUT LIKE A HAD. *(I made a Jule Nisse out of yarn. I wrapped the yarn around cardboard then I tied it and it turned out like a head.)*

They write about favorite stories and related projects:

THE VELVETEEN RABBIT IS LAFIT OUT BOAS THE BOY FARGAT HIM. *(left out because the boy forgot him.)*

They write about special events and field trips like our overnight camp-out on an island:

LAST NIT ME AND MI CLAS WESHT THE SUN SAT GO DONN IT WAS NISE THEN THE PEPOL MAD THE FIER AND WE TOSTED MARCHMALOS AND WE SAING SONG AND MY DAD PLAYD THE GATIR. *(Last night me and my class watched the sunset go down. It was nice. Then the people made the fire and toasted marshmallows and we sang songs and my dad played the guitar.)*

Units on such activities as hatching chicks take on new meaning as the children use their writing skills to document the events while they happen, and then later draw from their own notes as background for a personal narrative:

KATE HID TO PT TH CHIAK AN TO THE AKUDTE. *(Kathy had to put the chick [back] into the incubator.)*

The children write descriptive information about things they bring for "Show and Tell":

THIS IS A BEAR HEAD AND NY DAD MADE IT IN CUB SCOUS WHEN HE WUS UBOUT SEVINE YEARS OLD. HE GAVE IT TWO ME. PLEES DOO NOT TUCH! *(This is a bear head and my dad made it in Cub Scouts when he was about seven years old. He gave it to me. Please do not touch!)*

They write menus for snack time, signs, personal letters, and plays. They write notes requesting my attention when I am free or to inform me of a particular problem:

KATE, I NED TU TIK TU U. *(Kathy, I need to talk to you.)*

CEN WE CUNFRINS? *(Can we conference?)*

TARZ NO MORE YALLO PANT. *(There's no more yellow paint.)*

They write compliments about one another and describe social conflicts:

I DID NOT LIK WHEN GREG WUS TESING ME. *(I did not like when Greg was teasing me.)*

The children's responses to these diverse writing situations enable me to learn in more depth about the cognitive processes and thinking skills children bring to every learning situation. In addition to spelling, vocabulary, syntax and other aspects of language, their writing reveals the developmental levels of their understanding of causality, their intuitive logic, and their ability to engage in the so-called "higher" thinking processes. I discover that they can record observations:

SMAKEY WAS BITING HS LITL HOUSE MADE OUT OV A BOX. *(Smokey was biting his little house made out of a box.)*

write descriptions:

TODAY I SAW A KROW AND HEKOD THE KROW WAS OL BALCK AND THE HEKOD WAS A BLACK BAK AND WIT BRAST. *(Today I saw a crow and a chickadee. The crow was all black and the chickadee was black [with a gray] back and white breast.)*

make comparisons:

FOLS GOLD IS LINT BUT THE ROCK THENT HAS LI TL HALS IN IT IS 'HAVY.' *(Fool's gold is light but the rock with the little holes in it is "heavy.")*

I FOUND OUT THAT THE BALL OF CLAY WILL NOT DRAP WEN THE PENCILS ON IT. BUT IT WILL FALL WATH NO PENCILS.

predict:

THE LEVE IS GOWIN TO FAL ON THE BRD. *(The leaf is going to fall on the bird.)*

draw conclusions:

SMOKE IS WACHING TV AT MY HOWS. HE'S WACHING TOM AND JARE. HE DIDET SO AWA FRM THE TV SAD. I GAS HE LICS TV. *(Smokey is watching TV at my house. He's watching Tom and Jerry. He didn't go away from the TV set. I guess he likes TV.)*

establish cause and effect:

WAN YOU SKRH THE ROCK IT TN BLU IT TN BLU BCS THE NLL IS BLLW. *(When you scratch the rock it turns blue. It turns blue because the nail is blue.)*

and synthesize information to question and challenge each other:

THESE ARE THE SMOTH RACS I SOTED. BECH RAC. CRASTL. A FASL. THES ARE THE ROF FOCS I SOT. FOLS GOOLD. A FASL. BUT THE TREE [petrified wood] IS SMOTH AND RAF. WHY? *(These are the smooth rocks I sorted: beach rock, crystal, a fossil. These are the rough rocks I sorted: fool's gold, a fossil. But the tree is smooth and rough. Why?)*

In their educational lives children will be expected to write not only personal fiction and nonfiction but also fantasy, poetry, analyses, book reports, and scientific observations—the foundations for these can be laid in their first years of writing experience. Writing across the curriculum not only validates these different kinds of writing—it enables us to discover the individual strengths of student writers and the genres which highlight their talents. But, most important of all, it enables us to witness their competence as thinkers, even at the youngest age.

The Story and the "All About" Book

SUSAN SOWERS

In first-grade classrooms where stories dominate reading and writing, children may write stories exclusively. But if students read various types of books and teachers welcome many kinds of writing, teachers can expect other results. Beginners often delay writing stories while they explore a new, unassigned genre—the "all about" book. An "all about" piece of writing often has the phrase "all about" in the title and consists of a listlike collection of facts, features, and attributes of its subject. Steve's book, *Whales,* typifies "all about" writing.

Whales

Whales are black, and some are gray.
Whales are big. They can eat you in one bite.
There are brown whales, and there are black whales, too.
There are white whales.
There are blue killer whales.

Evidence for children's early preference for "all about" books comes from a collection of writing produced by Mary Ellen Giacobbe's first-grade class where her chief criterion for good writing was information and the children drew on their own experiences.

Steve, the author of *Whales,* was a student in Mrs. Giacobbe's class during her first year of teaching writing as a process. Before they made the transition from traditional instruction in October, the children wrote, when they were assigned, about a field trip or some other group activity. But after visiting another class, Mrs. Giacobbe decided to try letting the children take control of their writing. She put aside her lists of correctly spelled words and allowed the children to use invented spelling, because even though solicited from the children, the spelling words usually determined the topic and content of their writing and blocked the development of better ideas. Then, like older writers, the first graders learned to concentrate on content in first drafts and not on premature worries about correct spelling. Mrs. Giacobbe read her class several "books" written by members of the other first-grade class and set aside time and materials for writing. She arranged a writing area with a table and supplies of paper—large and small sheets, lined and unlined, loose and stapled into books between construction paper covers. She set out pencils, crayons, and markers for illustrations. After several weeks, all the children had experimented with unassigned writing, and some wrote every day. By the end of the school year, the twenty-two students had written over a thousand pieces.

Conferences were the heart of writing instruction. Mrs. Giacobbe conferred daily with children, responding to the content of their writing and briefly instructing them in a few skills. She also provided group conferences, a sharing time for work-in-progress and completed work. Each child selected only his or her best work to revise carefully for publication. Mrs. Giacobbe modeled the kinds of questions to ask a writer about content, and the children followed her examples and questioned each other. "What is your book about?" "And *then* what happened?" "How did you feel about that?" She insisted on self-evaluation: "What did you like about your book?" "Why do you want to publish this book more than the others?" "What is the best part of your book?" "Why?" An egocentric author could not assume for long that the audience had filled in information he or she had omitted. The children listened scrupulously and asked such questions as, "You said you played a game. Well, what game did you play?" or commented, "The part about the fourteen knots on the rope should go where you talk about *climbing* the rope, not at the end of the book." The authors usually acted on their classmates' suggestions. Far from being hurt by the scrutiny, they seemed to thrive on the close attention. Finally, Mrs. Giacobbe edited the spelling and typed the text of the individual book for publishing and adding to the class library.

The children wrote both stories and "all about" books. Many of the "all about" books resembled Steve's *Whales*, which is a partial inventory of his knowledge. He focuses mostly on color, but the information is not sorted into categories such as size, danger, kinds, and color in whales. He repeats sentence patterns: "Whales are" twice and "There are" three times. He provides some variation on "There are (color) whales" in the third repetition, when the color may have triggered the mention of another kind of whale: "There are blue killer whales." The forms both support and limit his content. Whether Steve wished to be famous among his classmates as an expert on whales or simply to display and order his knowledge for himself, we cannot be sure. We can be fairly certain that he was using a new medium— writing—to explore a new subject.

Clearly, *Whales* is not a story, not even a defective one. There is no narrative line, no chronological order. It belongs to another genre. To understand the "all about" piece and what it can reveal about its author, I first separated "all about" from other kinds of writing in Mrs. Giacobbe's class. When narrative elements were mixed in with an "all about" book, I counted the piece as a narrative if half of it or more was a narrative, that is, chronologically ordered events.

A tally of the 217 books published during the year showed that in November, the first month of publication, "all about" books were published twice as often as narrative, but by the end of the year, published narratives outnumbered "all about" books by three to one. Of the 36 books published in November, 13 were narratives and 23 were not. The percentage of published narratives increased throughout the months of first grade: November, 36 percent; December, 60 percent; January, 50 percent; February, 64 percent; March, 78 percent; April, 100 percent; May (and a few in June), 78 percent.

"All about" books raise the question of development. Since they appear earlier in the year than narratives, do they evolve into narrative, or are they an earlier form of nonnarrative writing, a forerunner of reports, arguments, and other expository writing? A few examples illustrate that both hypotheses may be true.

Two of Anna's books, both published in November, show how a young writer treated the same topic in two genres, first as an "all about" (*My Dog*) and then as a narrative (*My Bubble and My Dog*).

My Dog

I can't play with my dog until Christmas.
My dog jumped out of the truck and broke his leg.
I love my dog so, so much.
I do love my dog so, so, so, so much.
I had a friend come over. We watched the dog.
I do love my dog. I hugged the dog.

My Bubble and My Dog

I was blowing a bubble.
My dog jumped. She bit the bubble.
My dog hit the bubble. It got on her nose.
It got all over the house.
My mom was mad!

The first is effusive and repetitious. Three of the eight sentences are declarations of her love for her dog. The second illustrates her addition to an "all about" book of another feature young writers are learning, organization. The organization is chronological, unlike the earlier loose collection of statements, and many of the events are a consequence of the preceding one. She has left enough implicit (e.g., "It got on her nose. It got all over the house.") for most readers to construct a story. Her "all about" book appears a rehearsal for her story. But any story we piece together from the first is our own construction entirely, not Anna's.

Gary's books provide us with a different example of a young author's growth, this time within exposition. His first, published in November, is called *All About Alligators:*

Alligators eat people.
Alligators live in the water and on land.
Alligators sleep with their mouths open.
Alligators can open their mouths wide.
Alligators can swim.
They run quite fast on short, squat legs.

All About Alligators has 37 words. In May, Gary published a 339-word "all about" book which is organized into two parts, distinctive features of sailboats and categories of sailboats. Its length and elaboration set it apart from the earlier book. Although Gary expressed no feelings about sailboats, the voice of a thoughtful, well-informed six-year-old in this piece shows us his concern for boats and writing:

Sailboats

Sailboats don't go fast. But if the wind blows hard, they go faster.
The more sails there are, the faster it goes. Some sailboats are
small. And some are bigger than other ones.
Some sailboats can hold a lot of people and some can't.
Some sailboats tip over easily. If the wind hits the sail a different
way, it might tip over.
If a lot of people get on a small boat, it might tip over.
Catamaran is a kind of sailboat. It has four sails. It can't hold too
many people.
Catamarans can go fast because there are a lot of sails on them. It
is a racing boat. Some other sailboats can go fast, too.
Catamarans have a lot of sails because they are made that way. It
is hard to make the sail go the way of the wind.
The Constitution was a fighting ship. It has a lot of cannons. My
father has a copy of the blueprints of the Constitution.
The Constitution can hold a lot of people. Sometimes the Constitu-
tion was called Old Ironsides because when the cannon balls hit
it, they bounced right off.

He goes on in this fashion for another 150 words.

The growth visible in Anna's and Gary's work results from their addition of organization or length to the basic "all about" structure.

To further analyze the writing the first-grade children produced during that year, I examined the writing of four children. Chris, the only boy, and Sandy ranked high in academic achievement; Sarah was average; and Toni was lowest of all. In comparing their published and unpublished writing, I found these differences:

1. The four children matched the class trend of publishing more "all about" books early in the year, and more narratives later.
2. Each child was less regular and more uneven in his or her production of "all about" books or stories than the average for the class as a whole.
3. Almost every one of the four published each month.
4. Beginning in November, each wrote at least one narrative a month (except Toni in December).
5. Each wrote at least one "all about" book every month (except Sandy in February and April).
6. The four *wrote* far more "all about" books than stories in October, November, and December; from January on, they *wrote* almost an equal number of "all about" books and narratives. The same trend was not true for publishing.
7. The four *published* a higher percentage of narratives than the percentage they *wrote* (except Toni in November, Sarah in December, and Chris in March). Given a mixture of stories and "all about" books, the children came to favor stories as their best writing. When they began to write more stories in January, they published them even more often than before.

I examined in even more detail the writing of Sarah, the child who represented average academic achievement, although in many ways, she stands for no one but herself. She was also the most prolific writer in the class. Like the others, Sarah began the year with a strong preference for writing "all about" books and shifted during the second half of the year, when she wrote as many stories as "all about" books. In October and November, seven of her twenty-nine pieces, about 24 percent, were narratives. December 1 was a pivotal date in Sarah's writing development because her drawings, an important part of her rehearsal or prewriting behavior, changed. Suddenly, Sarah drew figures in profile. Humans, owls, and other characters could run, ride bikes, and chase each other. Where figures in profile appeared, they rehearsed action and often illustrated a narrative. Her forward-facing figures, static and motionless, often illustrated a nonnarrative. It is not clear whether her new drawing technique permitted greater scope in writing or whether her desire to write a story prompted these experiments in drawing actions.

On January 23, Sarah wrote *Me and Chipper*, typical of an "all about" book with affective content, in twelve minutes (eight minutes to draw the pictures and four minutes to write the words). This was a familiar routine to her by now, a self-assigned drill, a piece of writing she did not pursue into a final product. All fourteen figures in her drawings for *Me and Chipper* face forward. Here is the text of Sarah's almost automatic book:

Me and Chipper

Me and Chipper have lots of fun.
We have fun.
I love Chipper so much.
I won't stop loving Chipper.
It's so much fun.
It is fun.

In writing "The Pretty Little Girl" on January 11, Sarah rehearsed for each page by drawing eleven figures in profile with only one facing forward. The beginning of the story sounds as though the book will be another one in the *Me and Chipper* genre, but Sarah seemed to discover her antagonist, the villain, while drawing her heroine safely asleep at night:

The pretty little girl. Her name is Kristin.
She loves flowers the best. She hates school the worst.
She jumped up. She was scared. She saw the villain.
She punched him.
She's so glad. She's asleep.

Not only was Sarah's drawing related to the genre in which she wrote, but her other composing behaviors also fit the different types of products. For example, when narrative was new to Sarah, her activity level was high whenever she wrote narratives.

Graves (1979) has said, "When children try a new approach to writing, other areas in which they have been competent may suffer temporarily." Sarah's syntax suffered when she attempted narratives in November and December, and her spelling of easy, automatic words suffered a similar breakdown when she first began to revise drafts in the spring.

Sarah's composing process, then, is related to her production of either stories or "all about" books. When she explored narrative, she extended her rehearsal repertoire (drawing figures in profile and planning aloud), became restless while composing, and made syntactic errors in her text.

"All about" books present us with a puzzle. Why weren't the children's first pieces egocentric stories written in the first person, child-like, and full of stereotypical fun and fantasy? Instead we found rather serious, impersonal, listlike products, bold in their flat assertions about the domain of knowledge the author had staked out.

We can draw two conclusions from the children in Mrs. Giacobbe's class. First, they began writing mostly "all about" books, but gave way to a balance between the two. Second, they judged their own narratives to be their better books, fit for publication, at a much higher rate than their "all about" books throughout the year. The children seemed to have a double standard: one set of preferences for the actual practice of writing and another for judging the value of the product. Perhaps composing listlike books easily satisfied some desire the children (and all of us) had to order and display what they knew, while stories proved more satisfying to read. Later they may have learned to make their practice of writing accommodate their taste in reading. Surely, this is the beginning of the effects of reading on writing. Until this point, the benefits may have been in one direction only—encoding in writing enhanced decoding in reading.

The children's changing preferences also reflect the literate environments of home and school. The children had models for both narrative and nonnarrative writing. They knew stories from books, television, and conversation. Most of these children, from middle-class families, had heard concept books read to them. A potential model for the "all about" piece, a concept book, in Huck's (1976) classification of children's literature, is "one that describes the various dimensions of an abstract idea through the use of comparisons . . . a young child's information book" (p. 105–6). If the children imitated concept books, they fell short of exploring the dimensions of an abstract idea. However, each "all about" book was unified by a single subject, which may more accurately define concept books than the "abstract idea."

Mrs. Giacobbe's children did not invent the "all about" genre. Lesley Frost, daughter of the poet Robert Frost, kept journals as part of her schooling at home (1969). She learned to type at three, read at four, and composed essays at five. Although most of her entries in her first journal consist of narratives about the farm and surrounding woods in Derry, New Hampshire, a few resemble "all about" books. Many, in fact, have "about" in the title. The effects of her father's instruction in acquiring a "seeing eye" are evident in Lesley's use of specific details. "In our writing . . . we were learning to put the thing seen, heard, or felt on paper in words that made our parents sit up and take notice. If we brought Papa something born of a half a look, a glance, he sent us back for a whole look" ("Introduction," unpaged). Here is Lesley Frost's seventeenth entry in the journal she kept from February to June of 1905, written just before her sixth birthday. It resembles "all about" books in that the form seems to be a list of specific details.

Carol and Irma

Carol and Irma are such mischiefs that we don't know what to do but we have to stop them and when they don't stop we have to spank them and they cry they break dishes and cups and bend spoons and get hold of the sugar bowl and take a spoon and eat every bit of the sugar that is in it and they are great mischiefs.

Stories, for all the fascination they may hold for children and adults, do not lend themselves to imitation as readily as earlier theorists of children's writing development assumed. Britton, Burgess, Martin, McLeod, and Rosen (1975) write: "Probably the first written forms internalized are those of narrative, since anecdotes and stories, spoken and written, are part of a child's experience from the very beginning." Describing children who have taught themselves to write by writing stories, Britton (1982) states: "It would appear that the spoken language effectively meets young children's needs in general, and we must surmise that it is only as they come to value the written language as a vehicle for stories that they are likely to form an intention to write" (p. 163). These statements may echo our intuitions, yet the children in Mrs. Giacobbe's class prepared to write stories by writing unassigned "all about" books.

Not only have stories been presented as the natural starting point for writing, but they have also been presented as easy-to-write, beginners' stuff. In Moffett's (1968) rhetorical scheme, for instance, narrative occupies the bottom rung on the ladder, the least abstract form of writing. Moffett ignores the fact that even the most elementary stories are the result of many abstractions. A case could be made for a lower level of abstraction from which stories are developed; or for separate ladders of abstraction for narrative and nonnarrative writing.

Joan Didion, novelist and essayist, has written: "We live entirely, especially if we are writers, by the imposition of a narrative line upon disparate images" (1979, p. 11). She reminds us that stories must be constructed because there is no narrative line to events. Eudora Welty, in her autobiography (1984), tells of years of listening *for* stories as a child, a habit of attending to the world that nourished the novelist she was to become.

In contrast to Britton's and Moffett's explanations of the beginnings of writing, children do not begin to write exclusively with stories. Newkirk (1984), Bonin (1982), Matthews (1985), for example, have documented the nonnarrative writing which young children have done. Marie Clay (1975) found that five-year-old children beginning to write made lists of the letters, numbers, and words they knew. They spontaneously took inventory of their knowledge. "All about" books seem to be an elaboration in sentence form of the list-making of five-year-olds.

The first of our ancestors to write did not record oral stories or invent new ones to be written and read. Writing was first an administrative tool for keeping records. According to Jack Goody (1977), lists and catalogues are among the first written documents. Cole and D'Andrade (1982) find school a place where lists abound and agree with Goody that cognitive benefits accrue to the listers: "... [L]ists allowed new forms of inspection, because the representations were relatively fixed in time and space" (p. 24). The spirit of inventory-taking that the first graders enjoyed is apparently not new. "[S]chooling perpetuates the dream that Man could get a catalogue of all the world's contents, which when properly classified and memorized would represent full knowledge of the world" (p. 24).

Whatever the genre children write their first words in, the rest depends on the resources the class supplies to the child and the child's more solitary pursuit of resources, usually through reading. All this is not to say that "all about" writing is the most natural starting point for a writer, but simply to clear space for many starting points and to foster an appreciation of the role of reading in early writing. Lists, catalogues, and inventories—by word or by sentence—are congenial forms newcomers may invent for themselves.

References

Blackburn, Ellen. "Common Ground: Developing Relationships Between Reading and Writing." *Language Arts* 61 (October 1984): 367–75.

Bonin, Sandra. "Beyond Storyland: Young Writers *Can* Tell It Other Ways." In *Understanding Writing: Ways of Observing, Learning and Teaching,* ed. Thomas Newkirk and Nancie Atwell. Chelmsford, MA.: NEREX, Inc., 1982: 31–35.

Britton, James. "Spectator Role and the Beginnings of Writing." In *What Writers Know: The Language, Process, and Structure of Written Discourse,* ed. Martin Nystrand. New York: Academic Press, 1982.

Britton, James, Tony Burgess, Nancy Martin, Alex McLeod, and Harold Rosen. *The Development of Writing Abilities (11–18).* London: Macmillan Education, 1975.

Clay, Marie. *What Did I write?* Exeter, N. H.: Heinemann Educational Books, 1975.

Cole, Michael and Roy D'Andrade. "The Influence of Schooling on Concept Formation: Some Preliminary Conclusions." *The Quarterly Newsletter of the Laboratory of Comparative Human Cognition* 4 (April 1982): 19–26.

Didion, Joan. *The White Album.* New York: Simon & Schuster, 1979.

Frost, Lesley. *New Hampshire's Child: The Derry Journals of Lesley Frost.* Albany, N. Y.: State University of New York Press, 1969.

Goody, Jack. *The Domestication of the Savage Mind.* Cambridge: Cambridge University Press, 1977.

Graves, Donald H. What Children Show Us About Revision. *Language Arts* 53 (March 1979): 312–19.

Huck, Charlotte. *Children's Literature in the Elementary School.* New York: Holt, Rinehart and Winston, 1976.

Matthews, Kathy. "Beyond the Writing Table," this volume.

Moffett, James. *Teaching the Universe of Discourse.* Boston: Houghton Mifflin, 1968.

Newkirk, Thomas. "Archimedes' Dream." *Language Arts* 61 (April 1984): 341–50.

Welty, Eudora. *One Writer's Beginnings.* Cambridge: Harvard University Press, 1984.

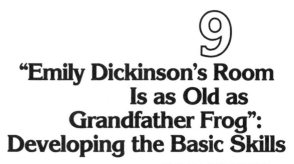

"Emily Dickinson's Room Is as Old as Grandfather Frog": Developing the Basic Skills

SUSAN BENEDICT

I stooped beside seven-year-old Kelly, observed her frown, and asked, "How's it going?" She squinted in a characteristic gesture and began to explain how she would write her piece about Emily Dickinson's house. Deliberate hand gestures emphasized her points.

"Well, I decided just to write about the rooms, rather than say she was born in 1830 and had a brother Austin and a younger sister Lavinia. Then I thought about Emily Dickinson's bedroom and I thought about the Thornton Burgess books we read, because Emily liked animals too. I decided to say, 'Emily Dickinson's room is as old as Grandfather Frog.'"

"That would really give the reader the feeling that it was very old," I said.

"Remember Susan (our guide) said *maybe* Emily Dickinson's spirit was still there," she continued. "That makes me shiver."

"How do you suppose the spirit would describe our visit?" I asked.

Kelly's eyes widened. "Maybe I could write it that way."

This brief conference was a result of research, reading, questions, visits, conferences, and more questions on the part of Kelly and her classmates. The seeds of her piece were planted three weeks earlier when she and her twenty second-grade classmates began their investigation of our community, Amherst, Massachusetts.

Perhaps the story starts even before that. Kelly and sixteen of her classmates had begun to view themselves as authors two years before, when I was their kindergarten teacher. In their first-grade year they deepened their understanding of the writing process in another writing process classroom. Writing was not new to these children. They expected to write daily.

I began the year determined that the children and I would grow as writers. I believed that the language arts should be incorporated in the content areas. As the year progressed, I became even more convinced that there is an inseparable relationship between the content area subjects and the language arts. It is virtually impossible to pursue one without the other. Reading and writing need content.

The Amherst project was part of a year-long focus on the concept of community. I could include their final drafts, but that isn't the story. The portfolio of experiences, notes, questions, false starts, and rumpled paper that moved the work to a finished state is the real story.

We began very close to "home," investigating our school community because it was a place where most of the children had already spent two years and considered themselves authorities. There were stories here. The children were surprised when their talk and shared observations led to questions. They were curious about the repair to the roof that disturbed their work. What did our principal *really* do? Why did men cut down the trees in the courtyards?

I asked questions too. I had known Mrs. Peters, our health room aide, for fifteen years, but I realized I knew very little about her or the daily working of the health room. That realization helped me to begin to define my own topic. The children likewise identified subjects and places they wished to know more about. We discussed what we already knew. I talked along with the children about the health room and Mrs. Peters, welcoming their information and experiences. Later I raised questions:

What kind of training did Mrs. Peters need to do her job?
How could she tell if kids were faking?

I was careful to frame questions that could not be answered by a quick yes or no, and I pointed that out to the children.

These questions would form the basis for my interview. Then, the children wrote down their questions. Finally we were ready to interview. The children accompanied me to the health room as silent partners. I interviewed Mrs. Peters and took notes to help me remember. The children then made appointments for their interviews.

Beatrix asked the principal, "Why are they fixing the roof?"

Her notes revealed his explanation: "it is liking (leaking)." Originally she wrote just that in her draft. Her classmates suggested she add more about the roof. Beatrix was able to observe the repair progress daily before school, at recess, and from inside the classroom. Her knowledge expanded, as her second draft shows (see page 85).

One October morning we went to the fields and woods surrounding our school community. Beatrix located flowers and three times called to the group, "Flowers are food for bees!" On the way back to the school she took her thumb out of her mouth long enough to fill me in on her knowledge of bees. "Bees get nectar and then make honey," she explained.

"Do you know anything else about bees?" I inquired.

"Well, they sting, you know!"

they. are fixing the
Roof Rolin is halping
there is ALAt to do.
A dog gos up on the Roof
and wachis the mann wrke.
it is A Big gob because
it is A big roof. it is hard
wrke. it is not ese. they
mke Alat of nowys
fxing the roof. we see
man on the roof alat
we hear nosis like
sowns of drls hamr's chane saw
and we her one man
giving instroksshns it is lowd nosy
and it mks a tarabl
sawna its orle and I hate
it. And I thik "you wd to it"

"If you wanted to find out more about bees what could you do?"

"I could look in books," was her immediate response. Later that day, Beatrix, the class, and I visited the school library to locate books about bees and other local animals. We were beginning to learn library skills by using the library for a real purpose.

Beatrix began reading. I showed how I took notes that might be useful to me in my writing. Because these children are authors themselves it was clear to them that someone else had written these books. We could learn from another's ideas, but the writing had to be ours. An excerpt from Beatrix's notes revealed the following:

When bees are
wong they go to
bee school. At bee
school the bees
lrne to tell the
hives apart.

Bees
dans to talk to the
athr bees.
talking thy dans.
Bees hav honny

She personalized and expanded this information in her draft. She used wording she had earlier crossed out.

> I also
> know that
> sintse stoudy
> bees. The
> sintses dascavrd
> that uong bees
> go to bee school
> in bee school
>
> the bees lrd to
> tell the hivse
> apart.
> ended of the
> Bees lalking
> each wathr they
> danc. the slower
> that the bee dances
> the farlhr away the
> nextr is.

She also incorporated her prior knowledge, which was expanded through research.

> Bees hav honny
> sacks on there
> lags. Bees get
> nactr from the
> flawrs then Bees
> make the nektr into
> honny.

Late in the year Beatrix revealed her understanding of how reading and note-taking could help her writing when she explained, "Well, first what I do is look for something I want in my report and if I find it I write something that would just sort of remind me what it is." She was alert not only to the help she could receive from books but also the need to maintain ownership of her own writing.

Beatrix and her classmates were developing tools to expand their writing experiences. When they needed them, they would, as Donald Murray (1984) says, take these tools out of their writer's tool box.

At other times I would structure activities. For example, I exhibited five different live animal communities in the classroom for a month. The children spent at least a half hour each day watching them. Many children went to the library to find information from an authority on the subject. Beatrix observed two of the communities and made the following notes:

In early February I focused the children's attention on the Amherst community. First the children needed to become aware of the wealth of treasures within our community. We began by brainstorming: Which member of our community would we investigate?

For a week the children wrestled with decisions about topics. They discussed possibilities at home, read the local papers, talked with me, and negotiated with each other.

Kelly, Sara, and Elizabeth were delighted to discover that Emily Dickinson was a former Amherst resident. They decided that Emily Dickinson and her house would be their topic for investigation.

We developed a plan. I would arrange for the children to visit the different locations and people they had chosen to investigate within the community. Meanwhile, they would research their topics to learn as much as they could before these visits.

Kelly, Sara, and Elizabeth spent mornings in the school library reading Emily Dickinson's poetry and biographies about her. They took notes to help them compose a letter to their guide revealing the information they already had, and asking questions that still remained.

The afternoon of the visit to the Dickinson house finally arrived. Laden with camera, tape recorder, clipboards and pencils we set off for the appointment. Susan, our guide, met us at the door looking like Emily herself. She was attired in a white dress, which was probably rescued from a local antique shop. She stopped before a portrait of three children and inquired, "Who do you think these children are?"

"That's probably Austin," said Elizabeth, pointing to the only boy.

"She must be Emily and the other one Lavinia because Emily was older," continued Kelly.

Susan smiled, "You're absolutely right."

She escorted us into the parlor. She was a skillful guide and made us all feel as if Emily might come down the staircase or lower some gingerbread from her bedroom window at any moment. Hanging on Susan's words, the children tried to cram all she said into their notes.

When we finally ventured upstairs to see the anticipated bedroom, the girls' eyes widened at the actual gingerbread basket they had read and heard about. There was an audible "Ah ..." when Susan gently lifted Emily Dickinson's dress from the closet.

"This is the very dress she wore," Susan explained.

"It's white," added Kelly.

"There's something unusual and unique about this dress. I want you to see if you can see anything on the front," Susan directed.

Kelly immediately noticed. "The pockets."

"Women's dresses in the mid 1800s didn't have big, square pockets on them. No one had them. Why do you suppose Emily Dickinson's dresses had big pockets?"

"For poems!" Kelly's face shone with surprise at the connection she'd made.

"I think she kept little scraps of paper in there and when she felt like writing a poem she would get her pencil out and she wouldn't forget or have to keep that line in her head," Susan hypothesized. Kelly remembered this.

The collecting was not yet complete. The following week I arranged for the class to visit the director of special collections at the local library. He would show us documents that were directly relevant to the children's individual investigations. Initially, we were directed to the second floor and escorted into the inner sanctum of the special collections. There we gathered around what looked like a library table from another century and pored over old documents and photographs while listening to the director's descriptions of Amherst in times past.

Kelly, Sara, and Elizabeth received an added bonus. They revisited Emily Dickinson's room through a doll-house-sized model on display at the library. They were now the authorities. They pointed out the gingerbread basket, the dress, and the sherry set which Elizabeth would later describe as "delicate as sherry itself." They relived their initial visit; stories poured forth to their classmates.

Several days later I observed Kelly frowning as she read what she had written. She was trying to create visual images of the rooms with her words, but her frowns revealed her dissatisfaction. Her piece lacked focus. Our sixty-second conference helped her to discover one.

"How do you suppose the spirit would describe our visit?" I asked.

Kelly's eyes widened. "Maybe I could write it that way." Her pencil moved across her paper.

> "Here they come!" I said to myself, "I wonder what ~~their~~ *their* names are" Susan, ~~their~~ *their* guide, asked just ~~before~~ I started <u>really</u> wondering

Kelly became Emily Dickinson as she wrote this piece. Although her notes were now tucked in her folder, she remembered them and wove selected facts into her writing (see page 90).

Susan's description of Emily Dickinson as "small as a wren and as bold as a chestnut burr" came from Kelly's reading. She added her remembered information about the dress pockets from her visit. She used poetic license when she quoted Susan: "The spirit of Emily Dickinson *is* still in the house." She connected with another writer when she wrote: "Emily Dickinson's room is as old as Grandfather Frog." She played with the spirit when she was "careful not to be in any of the pictures."

The theme of community was the thread that tied this school year together. At any particular time it became impossible to decide if we were studying oral language, reading, writing, science, or social studies. Our work developed more basic skills: thinking, questioning, and organizing. At each step along the way there was time: time to talk, time to observe, time to question, time to investigate *one* topic, time to think, time to read, time to write. As Donald Graves (1984) challenges, we must give children opportunities to specialize and sufficient time to work through projects. Only then will they have the skills to investigate wherever their imaginations and curiosities take them. It is only through such process-oriented learning that we and our children will develop the "real" basics.

"Emily Dickinson, Susan began, "discribed herself" 'As smallas a wren" and "bold as a Chestnut bur." "Thats right" I thogbt, 'I said that to almost everybody." The spirit of Emily Dickinson is still in the house." said Susan..." I sure am!" I thogbt.

Finally, Susan led the three girls to my room, I quickly ran up in front of them, to put away my poetrey. I made it, just in time too... As soon as I put away my pencil. they all came up the stairs |

"This room looks as old as grandfather frog." Kelly said.

"I should write that after they're gone." I thoght.

The girls and Mrs Benedict took pictures

but I was. was careful not to be in them. I returned upstairs and took out of my pocket a pencil. and paper and wrote: My room is as old as grandfather frog.

References   Graves, Donald H. "Writing Across the Curriculum." Speech, Amherst, Massachusetts, February, 1984.
Murray, Donald. *Write to Learn.* New York: Holt, Rinehart and Winston, 1984.

10

Children Re-create History in Their Own Voices

CORA FIVE
MARTHA ROSEN

"Silence." That was Quincy again. "Silence, silence. Mr. Adams will speak." Johnny twisted and turned and brought the whistle to his lips.

And suddenly there was silence. Johnny guessed there were many in that crowd who, like himself, were hanging on those words. Seemingly, Mr. Adams was calmly accepting defeat, dismissing the meeting for now he was saying,

"This meeting can do nothing more to save the country."

Johnny gave his first shrill blast on his whistle, and he heard whistles and cries seemingly in all directions, Indian war whoops and "Boston Harbor a teapot tonight!" "Hurrah for Griffin's Wharf!" "Salt-water tea!" "Hi, Mohawks, get your axes and pay no taxes!"

Fifth-graders enter the chaotic, and often frightening world of pre-Revolutionary Boston when they share the experiences of apprentice-silversmith Johnny Tremain. We will show how these students used children's literature when they researched their American history reports to help them experience the colonists' conflicts. The characters from their reading remained alive in the students' later reports.

To promote an immersion in reading as preparation for writing, students discuss fictional works. One day, when the group gathered to talk about their selections, they debated the role played by the Sons of Liberty:

Responding to Literature

Marcia said, "They were a group of men who were against England. . . ."

Mark interrupted, "I know. Wasn't John Hancock one of them?"

"They made a plan that they would throw the unloaded tea into the harbor," Linda added excitedly.

Greg interjected, "Gee, these guys like Paul Revere and Sam Adams were acting like criminals. Weren't they breaking the law?"

On another day, they described the uses of a hornbook in the "dame school" which Kit Tyler and her cousin Mercy established in their home in *The Witch of Blackbird Pond*. And, in another discussion, they talked about *The Slave Dancer* by Paula Fox. On that day, Steven admitted sheepishly, "I couldn't finish the book. The things that happened on that slave ship were too awful. I felt sick reading about it." These discussions help keep the books alive for the students.

Selecting Topics

All members of the class read several fiction and nonfiction books prior to choosing a report topic. They also view filmstrips and films, and listen to cassettes. Then each begins to focus on a specific topic of interest, such as the colonial shoemaker, the Salem Witch Trials, the Boston Tea Party, or school discipline, all subjects having to do with Colonial America. For the next few weeks, they learn as much as possible about their particular topics.

Whatever the report topic they choose, each class member reads at least three, and sometimes as many as eight, books for background. As Lucy Calkins (1980) suggests, they read short, easy books first and then move on to more difficult material. Especially useful books are Jean Fritz's biographies of colonial patriots, the "Life in Colonial America" series published by Troll Associates, and Leonard E. Fisher's "Colonial Craftsman" series. Those students interested in witchcraft delve into additional historical fiction, such as *Witches' Children* by Patricia Clapp and *The Visionary Girls* by Marian Starkey.

Encyclopedias are consulted in the final stages, but only to check such details as dates, customs, school hours, or geographical descriptions.

As they finish each book, all students compile rough bibliographies in their journals. They also write in their journals while they are reading, or after completing a book (Tchudi and Tchudi, 1983), to record interesting facts, opinions, feelings, and ideas. For example, after reading about colonial shoemakers, a student wrote in his journal, "I can't believe that shoemakers pulled teeth. I didn't know that. I don't think I'd want to go to one." This fact became part of his lead in his final report.

Brainstorming Information

When the students have become "experts" in their fields of interest, they brainstorm. In conferences, they teach a partner about their topic, as Alix did one day. "You mean, they *really* used dunce caps?" squeals Jennifer. "Yeah," explains Alix. "If the students didn't know their lessons, they didn't always get whipped. Sometimes they would have to sit on a dunce stool and wear a dunce cap and a sign that said, "Baby-Good-for-Nothing."

On the other side of the room, Nathan taught two friends about shipbuilding. "Do you know what they used for building those ships? They used tools that had to be made by hand like an adz." "What's an adz?" asked John. "Here, it looks like this," responded Nathan, drawing a quick illustration. "It was used for sharpening wood." The whole room hums with accounts of the Boston Massacre, colonial games, and whaling.

After these brainstorming conferences, the children write down every-thing they know about their subject, using only one side of the paper. They include questions and facts they need to know. If they cannot think of words or dates, they leave blank spaces to fill in later. The purpose of this activity is to write everything they can remember.

Drafting Ideas

During the next writing session, they review these drafts and look for two or three subtopics or chapters. They place these chapter headings on separate sheets of paper. Then the students take their original drafts and cut them up, taping all parts having to do with one chapter on the appropriate page in any order. They also include any questions or facts they want to learn. They read through their journals and recopy their thoughts, interesting facts, and opinions on the correct chapter page. Jamie's notes for a chapter on "What Happened" for his "Boston Tea Party" read:

What happened

The Boston tea party was an
act in which England taxed the tea.
342 cases of tea were dumped into the water
broke on board 3 ships   The D
that had tea in their hulls.
they broke the boxes and cut through the canvas and dumped the
tea overboard
they went into the water and found a
problem the water was to shallow and the tea was stacking
up like hay. So they splashed the tea around.

When they have finished this activity, the students are ready for fur-ther research. Now they use encyclopedias to find the answers to spe-cific questions, although they continue to read trade books. Their re-search is conducted mainly in the school library. Following the recommendation of Lucy Calkins (1980) we asked them to adhere to the rule established in the classroom: they cannot read and write at the same time. Once they discover information, they read it, turn the book over, and write it down in the proper chapter. When they have finished gathering additional information, they are ready to write again.

The students take each chapter separately and treat it as a personal writing piece. Since the first draft of each chapter is disorganized, they reorder information, add supportive details, work on leads, and develop strong endings. For example, John used his journal entry about the colonial shoemaker as dentist in this lead to one chapter:

Not only did the colonial shoemaker pull teeth, make saddles and harnesses, he made his own tools.

He concluded that the shoemaker had to be a very talented man.

Conferring for
Response

The children confer often with each other and with each of us. Because they are experts on their topics and frequently know more than we do, we listen. We ask questions when we don't understand. Conferences often take the form of discussions, as the children explore their ideas about representation, slavery, authority, independence, and revolution.

The following conference occurred one day in class. Jennifer, looking puzzled, said, "I don't understand. It would have been so easy for England to let the colonists have one—just one—little representative in Parliament. Why were they so stubborn?"

Carl explained, "The King wanted to have power over the colonies. He didn't want to give in to their demands. The colonists were supposed to be loyal English subjects."

Debbie joined in, "Yeah, well, the colonies thought that being taxed for the French and Indian War wasn't fair. So they formed the First Continental Congress."

Jennifer asked, "What was that?"

"It was a meeting where people were chosen from each colony. They met together to decide what to do about the taxes of the King," answered Alexis. "At least *there* they thought representation was important!"

Carl questioned, "Didn't they write a letter to King George?" Alexis responded, "Yeah, the Continental Congress wrote a letter to the King telling him not to listen to his bad advisors."

Jennifer concluded, "So the colonists really tried to do things peacefully at first, but Parliament wouldn't listen. If England had given in just a little bit, there might not have been a war."

Carl laughed, "Letters sure didn't work, did they?"

"Well, at least they tried. They even had to have a Second Continental Congress later when they decided to declare their independence," Alexis informed his friends.

The ideas the students express in these conferences help them to take a position in their reports, such as this one of Jamie's:

One thing I found interesting above all was that not one ounce of tea was stolen. That way England could not call it robbery, but it could be called a demonstration.

Mindy expressed her feelings about the Salem Witch Trials:

Nineteen unlucky people got hanged. It was stupid and terrible what they did to these innocent people. Children were left homeless and many people died in jail of sickness and starvation ... Now you can imagine what a fix those girls were in. If they confessed the real reason—that they were pretending—they would get in so much trouble. If they lived in our days they would get grounded for five years. But, on the other hand, if they didn't confess, more people would get hanged and hurt.

Alexis examined the military situation in the colonies and the importance of the Second Continental Congress in organizing the rebellion:

The Second Continental Congress encouraged people in the colonies to fight in the war against England. The Congress had to have a General and a real army, not one with farmers, storekeepers and boys. Almost all the people in the army didn't have any experience. The Congress chose George Washington as the general of the army because of his experience. Would he be able to defend the Declaration of Independence?

When students complete their revisions, they have editing and proofreading conferences. They work for more precise, vivid language that will make their reports clear, interesting and lively, such as this excerpt from Jamie:

Publishing and Sharing

The Night the Revolution Began:

The Boston Tea Party Prologue

"What? This is preposterous! Who do they think they are saying 'No taxation without representation!'" shouted King George, the III. "After all we did for them during the French and Indian War, the least they can do is pay their taxes! I know what I'll do. I'll show them who has the power to make taxes. I'll put a tax on tea. They all love tea. From this day forward all American colonists must pay a tax on tea."

This and other unfair taxes brought on the Boston Tea Party on December 16, 1773.

The Boston Tea Party

The night air was still as about 200 men and boys dressed as Mohawk Indians hurried down back alleys toward three ships waiting in Boston Harbor ...

The writing style of these writing process students differs markedly from the encyclopedia-like reports we received from fifth-graders three years ago. Since learning to use the process of writing, our students have written reports that sound like themselves, rather than the *World Book*. They are also more enthusiastic and involved. As one student expresses it:

> *I love doing reports this way. I know a lot about the Boston Tea Party. Last year my report on the heart was 20 pages long. I copied it all from the* World Book *and* Encyclopedia Britannica—*and I didn't learn a thing about the heart!*

They recopy carefully in pen, make a table of contents, illustrations and a cover, a title page and a full bibliography. Some of the titles of their reports are "At Home in Colonial America," "Colonial Schools and Discipline," and "Blacksmiths and Their Work." The crucial years of the Revolution come alive in "The Night the Revolution Began: The Boston Tea Party," "The Second Continental Congress," and "The Battle of Yorktown." They address the issue of slavery in "Harriet Tubman and Her Secret Route to Freedom," and "Road to Freedom." Finally, they share their reports with their friends, using their own voices to recreate history.

References

Calkins, Lucy. Information from workshops with teachers, 1980.

Clapp, Patricia. *Witches' Children: A Story of Salem.* New York: Lothrop, Lee and Shepard, 1982.

Forbes, Esther. *Johnny Tremain.* Boston: Houghton Mifflin, 1943.

Fox, Paula. *The Slave Dancer.* Scarsdale, N. Y.: Bradbury Press, 1973.

Speare, Elizabeth. *The Witch of Blackbird Pond.* Boston: Houghton Mifflin, 1958.

Starkey, Marian. *The Visionary Girls: Witchcraft in Salem Village.* Boston: Little, Brown, 1973.

Tchudi, Stephen and Susan J. Tchudi. *Teaching Writing in the Content Areas: Elementary School.* Washington, D.C.: National Education Association, 1983.

11
Querer Es Poder

CURTIS W. HAYES
ROBERT BAHRUTH

Pearsall, Texas, the home of the world's largest peanut, is a small rural community sixty miles south of San Antonio. Primarily agricultural, the region attracts and employs Mexican-American migrant laborers, who work long hours in the hot Texas sun for low wages. Few of these migrants can either read or write; at best they are semiliterate. Although migrant families would like to remain in Pearsall for the full school term—late August through late May—many cannot. They come to Pearsall after school begins in the fall and leave before it closes in May, taking their children with them.

By the middle of September our class consisted of twenty-two migrant children. Their ages, ranging from ten to sixteen, revealed that some had already failed a year, a few more than one. They spoke Spanish, their first language, in the home, on the job, and on the playground. Most knew little English. Their only exposure to English came from television, the radio, and from school. Their reading abilities were also limited: most were reading three or more years below grade level. Some were nonreaders. If the trend held, many of our children would be illiterate dropouts by the end of their ninth year in school and would become migrant laborers, like their parents, following the maturing of the crops from one region to another, year by year. Few of our children had any hopes, desires, or dreams that they considered attainable.

The skills needed to read and write English were just two sets of skills our children lacked, but they needed these skills most if they were to have success in school. We believed we should develop their reading and writing skills simultaneously. "Develop" is a key concept, for we among others (Cummins 1981, 1983; Krashen 1981, 1982), believe that reading and writing develop along a continuum. However, it is much more difficult to learn to read and write in a second language than it is to learn to use a second language for speaking and listening (Cummins, 1981). Speaking and listening skills are usually used in a rich context; both participants in a conversation, for example, are face to face. They share a common purpose, they know what they want to say and have some idea of the response and they speak from experience—usually a shared or personal experience (Britton 1972; Smith 1982). It was this experience that we hoped to tap—the accumulated knowledge of years past that students bring with them to the classroom. This experience is at the heart of student interest and was more meaningful to our children than the material in texts. Writing from experience, from the known, was crucial.

Improving Self-Concept

We began in August, when our students—strangers to us and we to them—trickled into our classroom. We found them unable to perform many of the tasks we set before them. They reflected a host of negative attitudes and could not become good students unless they saw themselves as a community of learners. The format of our class needed to be revised. We began working together with our children on projects to raise their self-esteem and to give them a sense of unity. We traced each other's silhouettes using an opaque projector. We measured each other's armspans and heights and recorded our findings. We traced our hands and wrote some of our favorite things on each finger. We designed personalized covers for our first dialogue journals. Many of these activities were enjoyable art experiences. They encouraged cooperation and involved just the slightest amount of reading and writing.

These activities had no wrong answers and thus contained no threat of failure. Each provided the opportunity for success, and the effect of a string of successes began to appear. Our students' actions and language started to show signs of well-being. At the same time, we wanted our children to see us less as threats and more as facilitators. Therefore, for each activity we included ourselves in teams with the students. Our classroom became an incubator where self-esteem and cooperation were allowed to grow.

Hooked on Books

We also read aloud to our students daily. Each day we read one or two of our favorite stories and afterwards, we discussed them. We began with easier, high-interest stories our children could relate to; gradually we increased the level of complexity and length.

When we read a book, we wrote its title on construction paper and put it on the bulletin board. During the sixth week, each child picked one of the forty titles we had read and illustrated a scene from the story. Then using the illustration as a prop, the child told the story to the class. This oral language activity met with success. Our children had acquired knowledge, language, and confidence and were involved in a task that was not threatening. At the same time, and throughout the year, our children acquired story grammars which enabled them to predict the drift of the stories we continued to read to them (Carrell, 1983). The reading hour soon became a quiet hour around which the rest of our day revolved.

In this way we planted and nurtured the seed of reading and it showed signs of germination early on. Our children began to ask permission to take home books we had read to them as well as paperbacks we had purchased for our class library. They elected a class librarian and on Fridays, we chose four or five of the new books and introduced them to the class by discussing the title, the author, and the dedication page. Then we would read the first few pages aloud. At a point of high interest we closed the book and asked if anyone wanted to take the book home over the weekend. There were always more hands than we could accommodate, and the ones we selected were looked upon with envy. Books assumed a new meaning and became valued commodities.

Next, we introduced dialogue journals (Staton, 1980, 1983; Shuy, 1980). The students wrote their journal entries on topics of their choice. We read the entries and responded within these guidelines: we neither criticized content nor did we edit. Most of our children accepted this way of writing to us and were eager to read what we had written.

Dialogue Journals

Others, however, seemed reluctant to write anything. Larry, for instance, when first asked to write submitted a blank sheet. Our response was: "How can we answer you if you don't write?" Larry's answer was, "I don't like writing." We responded, "Does anything bother you about writing?" He answered [all dialogue entries are unedited]:

"I don't like to write because I can't not spell right. that's whats bother me about writing."

We replied:

"Don't worry about it right now. The more you read and write the better your spelling will get. Just worry about getting your ideas written down; then you can circle words and check your spelling when you finish."

Apolinar expressed mixed feelings about writing in his first entry:

I like writing because we do art on it sometimes an I love writing and reading books because I love stories and I love draw in pictures alot because you can learn to draw pretty pictures and writing to other people and i hait writing what the teacher said to us to do because i like to write wat i like to do at my paper.

Apolinar had something to say, not only to us, but to all of his teachers, and he expressed himself well. We advised him:

You should keep a list of ideas about topics you want to write about. Keep it in your writing folder. Then when it's time to write you'll have plenty to write about. Why don't you try writing on your own, without our telling you to write?

Both Larry and Apolinar capitalized on the dialogue they could share with us. Eventually, their daily entries increased to one or more pages. Our children persevered in getting their thoughts down on paper. We learned that they would write if emphasis was placed on meaning and communication. Reading and writing, our children were to learn, were matters of increasing returns; the more they read and wrote, the easier those tasks became.

The students wrote about topics other than school. For example, Francisco wrote:

I can just bat to the left and sometimes I bat to the right and in the mittle to. Yesterday we play baseball it was Larry and Augustin agents Luis and me and we hit first and I hit first and I do a home-run and we win the skore was 12 to 4 that why we win and we hit hord that why we win and they slow and we make homerun.

Our response:

We guess you know how to bat to the left, right and middle then. Maybe we can play against Mrs. Gallagher's class. I can hit home-runs too!

The dialogue journals involved them with a real, responsive audience: us. By writing, we demonstrated the importance of writing in both their lives and our lives. It is for this reason that Graves (Walshe, 1982) argues: "The writing teacher, like the pottery teacher, must practice the craft alongside the students." And we continued to do so throughout the year.

Our responses showed native speaker competence and provided accuracy in form and structure. Our children who were fluent, but not accurate, needed a model. We provided accurate spellings, structures, and forms. Jaime wrote one day that it was "harad" to hit a baseball. A portion of our response included the correct spelling of hard: "Why is it so hard," we asked? Jaime spelled "hard" correctly in his answer.

The dialogue journal also provided a reading lesson each day, a conversation between two readers who are also writers, each writing for the other, and each reading what the other has written. Hatch (1983) suggests that language learning consists of learning how to carry on a conversation: and we believe that growth in writing and reading is enhanced by such an interchange, a conversation. Norma Alicia's confidence in herself as a reader shows in this entry:

Well yesterday I help to him [her brother] in math and words in English I have some books and yesterday I help brother in math and words in Englis. I like help us because I like teacher and is beautiful for me yesterday I talk with my mother and father and my mother said, Mr. Bahruth said you paint pretty Why you don't study for painter and I said I want to study for teacher and she said o.k. what every you want that's fine o.k. Do you have much of books?

Our response:

Many high schools have teachers who just teach art and how to paint. You could study to be an art teacher. I have lots of books at my house. My children already have lots of books too!

The reading/writing connection continued as our children asked questions and made comments about books.

AMY: *Can you read us a book about Charlotte's wed on Monday Charlotte's wed is a good book thier are 22 chapters and it was writhen by E.B. White and the author Stuart Little and Pictures by Garth Williams*

PATRICIA: *Are you gonna be her in Pearsall in Ester. Do you live in a traille. What is gonna be are next book?*

Sometimes we asked questions about books and they answered us:

Florencia, did you get any books for Christmas? What did you read over the holidays? We read three long books.

FLORENCIA: *I forgot to tak one home but my brother took one hom. And I read it all and it was a long book and my other brother took a book to and I read it to my cousin. And I ame going to tack the new books' you braut yesterday. I read two books to my mother and cousin and they lik them and my father read it himselfe and he told me he like it. And he told me to tack a book hom.*

They also wrote about writing:

GILBERT: *I been wondorwen if we can make a book about some dreams.*

JESSICA: *Why do you tell us to write alot and you write a little bit?*

Our response:

You have to remember that we write answers in 22 journals every day. Do you still think we don't write a lot?

In previous years, writing had tended to be a "No" world of rules, corrections, and often artificial—and thus hard to follow—prescriptions that had little to do with natural expressiveness. However, in their journals our students encountered a "Yes" world, where they were encouraged to take risks (Rico, 1983). The exchanges brought our children and us to a common understanding. We were both learning, both teaching, both nonjudgemental, both caring and sharing individuals. As a result, the confidence of all increased.

Our children abandoned the "defensive" posture they brought to our classroom as we learned that "school is where the children are and the teacher must systematically share their lifeways" (Rosenfeld, 1971).

Let Their Ink Flow Freely

Teachers are worried over errors, and we were no exception. Our children exhibited a number of them; but we seldom had errors which obscured meaning. We still did not correct or draw attention to errors as such. Many of the errors that appeared in their journals were developmental errors, common to children not yet competent in English, their second language (Paulston, 1974). The errors are not a cause for alarm, and teachers should not correct them. Children learning English as a second language will make errors, but as they become more proficient, as their production increases, as they read and write more, the number of errors will decrease. But, they will not disappear overnight. If children did not make errors they would not be learning.

Once the Walls Are Removed

Journal writing provided the bridge of confidence between our children and both of us. Journal writing also built an additional bridge, a bridge that led into the kinds of expository writing and reading that our children were expected to do in school. We continued the journals, but we added writing folders for our children, as well as for ourselves, and we all began writing. We first assigned semicontrolled, ten-minute writing tasks (see Kirby and Liner [1981] for a complete list of these activities) such as:

I get really angry when . . .
I'm most happy when . . .

Everyone could write on these topics. The short time frame again forced fluency rather than accuracy. Afterwards, we shared our experiences by reading to each other what we had written. We also responded to these experiences, often asking for clarification and additional information.

We carried this practice over to the *Troll Creative Writing Filmstrips*. At the end of each filmstrip were a series of photographs that we left projected on the screen while we wrote whatever came to mind. There were photographs of a chewed-up pencil, a horse running in a field, a kite shaped like a bird, and people with native clothing and interesting faces.

After each intense writing session we stored our drafts in our writing folders. We began to accumulate enough drafts to use for ideas for papers. And these papers soon evolved into ideas for books. The students selected and edited final papers, chose a theme, and compiled a book. In the first few books (*Abecedario, Limited Edition, Autumn Leaves,* and *The I Dare You Cookbook of Weird Recipes*), they wrote about topics they knew. Other early books also reflected personal or imaginary/fantasy themes: *Love Letters, Everything you always wanted to know about Aliens . . . but were afraid to ask.*

Then we began to integrate content areas into our writing:

International Alphabet Soups	(Social Studies)
Uncle Sam's Biography	(Social Studies)
Great Expectations	(Social Studies: career choices)
Small Wonders and Magic Machines	(Science)
Mother Nature's Tiny Wonders	(Science)

For *Small Wonders and Magic Machines*, students chose objects and natural phenomena to investigate. Apolinar's report on the attributes of the leg of the cockroach exemplifies the students' writing.

We suggested one theme: *The What Did U Say? Handbook of Idioms*. Shirley Brice Heath (1984) states that one handicap of children who come from nonmainstream homes is their lack of exposure to idioms. She points out that teacher talk can be highly idiomatic. Consequently, children who cannot comprehend idioms may appear to be "slow." We searched through the basals and we had the children bring to our attention any idioms they found in their reading. We also listed idioms we found in the books we read to them. We wrote our list (approximately eighty to ninety idioms) on the board and each student chose one or two. Then they acted out each expression and wrote the meaning in their own words. Next, they illustrated the literal meaning and wrote the actual, idiomatic meaning underneath the illustration (Figures 2 and 3).

FIGURE 1

MARCH 15, 1984   Science Report Apolinar Garcia
        The cock Roach leg

MATERIALS:

Cock Roach, glass slides, Paper, scissors, microscope,

PROCEDURE:

1) Carfully Remove the leg froom the cock Roach with 
2) Put the leg on the glass slide.
3) Put the slide on the projector microscope
4) turn on the projector microscope.
5) focus

RESUITS:

The leg of a cock Roach looks like a chicken
leg. It has alot of veins and hair.

The End of New Beginnings

Our students improved, often dramatically, in their use of the English language. Their ability to read and write improved as they continued to write about topics important to them as Jessica did with her piece on the peanut field (Figure 4).

We knew our children were improving just by being around them, and when they took their first test in December (administered by their Chapter I teacher) their scores indicated they were catching on and up. We evaluated them again during the latter part of April, when the district began to place students for the next grade level. Their scores and their distribution follow on page 106.

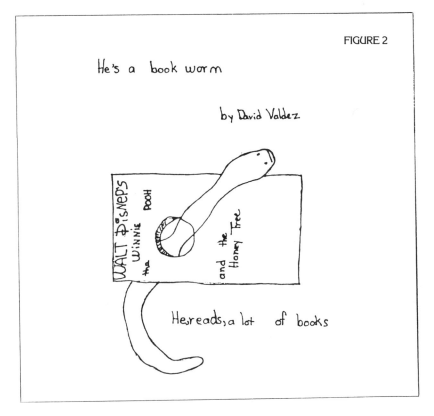

FIGURE 2

He's a book worm

by David Valdez

He reads, a lot of books

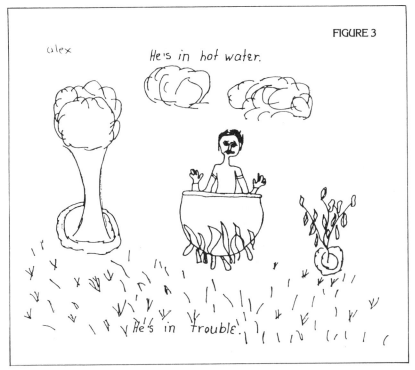

FIGURE 3

alex

He's in hot water.

He's in trouble!

FIGURE 4

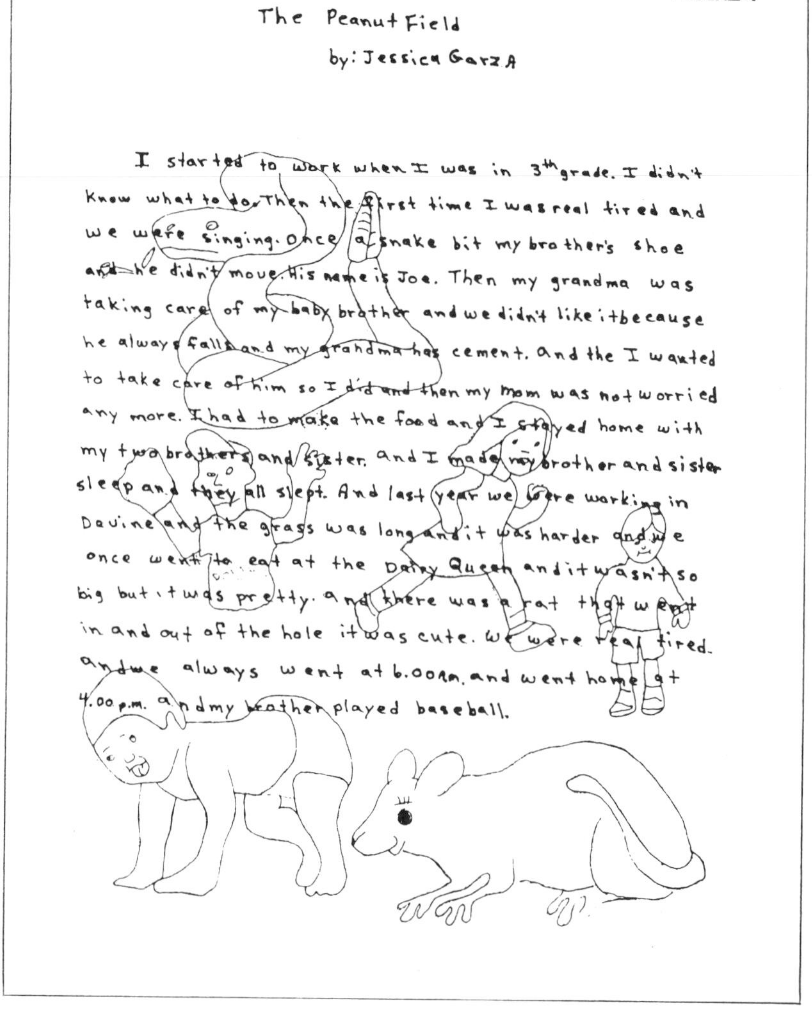

The Peanut Field

by: Jessica Garza

I started to work when I was in 3th grade. I didn't know what to do. Then the first time I was real tired and we were singing. Once a snake bit my brother's shoe and he didn't move. His name is Joe. Then my grandma was taking care of my baby brother and we didn't like it because he always falls and my grandma has cement. and the I wanted to take care of him so I did and then my mom was not worried any more. I had to make the food and I stayed home with my two brothers and sister. and I made my brother and sister sleep and they all slept. And last year we were working in Devine and the grass was long and it was harder and we once went to eat at the Dairy Queen and it wasn't so big but it was pretty. and there was a rat that went in and out of the hole it was cute. We were real tired. and we always went at 6.00 am. and went home at 4.00 p.m. and my brother played baseball.

One grade level improvement: one child
Two plus grade level improvement: seven children
Three plus grade level improvement: thirteen children
Four plus grade level improvement: one child

Even with this improvement, only six of our twenty-two children read, by the end of the year, at the fifth-grade level. Sixteen still tested below grade level. The Informal Reading Inventory is normed with a native speaker population, but the district required students to take this test as they would be "mainstreamed" in the fall. Yet these scores should in no way obscure the tremendous progress these children made. Our children now know they can learn; they have learned how to learn, and they are proud of their achievements. They look forward to the beginning of school in the fall.

Carrell, Patricia L. "Some Issues in Studying the Role of Schemata, or Background Knowledge, in Second Language Comprehension." Paper presented at 17th Annual TESOL Convention, Toronto, Canada, March 1983.

Graves, Donald H. *Writing: Teachers & Children at Work.* Exeter, N.H.: Heinemann Educational Books, 1983.

Goodman, K., Y. Goodman, and B. Flores. *Reading in the Bilingual Classroom: Literacy and Biliteracy.* Rosslyn, Va.: National Clearing House for Bilingual Education, 1979.

Hatch, E. M. *Psycholinguistics: a Second Language Perspective.* Rowley, Mass.: Newbury House, 1983.

Heath, Shirley Brice. Remarks made to the 18th Annual TESOL Convention, Houston, Texas, 1984.

Kirby, D., and T. Liner. *Inside Out.* Montclair, N.J.: Boynton/Cook, 1981.

Krashen, S.D. *Second Language Acquisition and Second Language Learning.* Oxford: Pergamon Press, 1981.

Krashen, S.D. *Principles and Practice in Second Language Acquisition.* Oxford: Pergamon Press, 1982.

Paulston, C. B. "Linguistic and Communicative Competence." *TESOL Quarterly* 8 (1974): 347–62.

Rico, G. *Writing the Natural Way.* Los Angeles: J. P. Tarcher, 1983. (Distributed by Houghton Mifflin Company.)

Rosenfeld, Gerry. "Shut Those Thick Lips!": *A Study of Slum School Failure.* New York: Holt, Rinehart and Winston, 1971.

Shuy, R. "ESL and the Reading and Writing Process." Lectures Presented to Second Annual ESL Institute, University of Texas at San Antonio, Summer 1980.

Smith, F. *Understanding Reading* (3rd Edition). New York: Holt, Rinehart and Winston, Inc., 1982.

Sowers, Susan. "Reflect, Expand, Select: Three Responses in the Writing Conference." In *Understanding Writing,* ed. Thomas Newkirk and Nancie Atwell. Chelmsford, Mass.: Northeast Regional Exchange, 1982.

Staton, J. "Writing and Counseling: Using a Dialogue Journal." *Language Arts* 57 (1980): 514–18.

Staton, J. "Dialogue Journals: A New Tool for Teaching Communication." *ERIC/CLL News Bulletin* 6 (1983): 1–2; 6.

Sucher, F. *Individual Reading Inventory.* Oklahoma City: Economy Book Company, 1978, 1982.

Walshe, R. D., ed. *Donald Graves in Australia.* Exeter, N.H.: Heinemann Educational Books, 1982.

PART THREE
THE AGE OF REFLECTION

"On the Inside Where It Counts"

THOMAS NEWKIRK

In eighth grade I worried constantly about my hands—worried about how they looked. Were the veins on the backs of my hands too prominent? Were my fingernails clean? too obviously bitten? In the winter my fingers looked bluish at the beginning of the day. I could, and sometimes did, put my hands in my pockets, but that looked, well, "strange" and anything was better than looking "strange." I was even sensitive about appearing sensitive.

This fastidiousness would have surprised my fifth-grade teacher, for that year I wore the same shirt for eighty straight days, forcing my mother to give it a quick wash when *she* insisted it needed cleaning.

I had become *self-conscious*. Say it quickly and it is a weakness, implying unnecessary nervousness. But say it slowly—self . . . consciousness and it's something more positive, perhaps the major achievement of the adolescent years. Howard Gardner, a developmental psychologist, writes:

It is necessary for the (adolescent) to come to terms with his own personal feelings, motivations, and desires—including sexual ones which are his lot for having passed puberty. There may also be considerable pressure—and desire—to think about one's emerging sense of self. (Gardner, 1983: 251)

Much of this thinking is kept private, just as my concern for my hands was a closely guarded secret. In effect, I began living two lives, one which was revealed to everyone and one which was locked within. Like most adolescents I felt the pressure of my own secrets.

Just as adolescents struggle to discover who they are, the schools they attend have also had identity problems. Since World War II we have been segregating young adolescents, first in junior high schools, and more recently in middle schools. These schools have often had difficulty defining a distinct mission, one separate from the elementary schools these students have left and the high schools they will enter. Even the names—*middle* school, *junior* high school—suggest unclear purposes. But in these years a kind of awareness emerges, a kind of personal intelligence, that can become a focus of language education.

This new concern for the inner life is evident in the fiction that begins to become popular in early adolescence. For example, in the award-winning novel, *From the Mixed-Up Files of Mrs. Basil E. Frankweiler*, two children learn about the value of secrets. Claudia and her younger brother Jamie run away from their home and spend several days in the Metropolitan Museum of Art, where they try to determine whether a statue, attributed to Michelangelo, is authentic. They finally take a trip to see Mrs. Frankweiler, who had donated the statue, and in her files they find the answer to their question. But the clever Mrs. Frankweiler knows that Claudia will keep this secret. For with this secret, she will be able to return home different.

Returning with a secret is what she really wants ... Claudia doesn't want adventure. She likes baths and feeling comfortable too much for that kind of thing. Secrets are the kind of adventure she needs. Secrets are safe, and they do much to make you different. On the inside where it counts. (150)

Students also begin—or can begin—to explore this inner life in their writing.

I'll first define more precisely what I mean by self-consciousness and then examine the part it plays in Katherine Paterson's *Bridge to Terabithia*. Finally, I will show how students begin to use self-consciousness in the stories they write.

The self-conscious writer develops three special capacities to perceive and depict characters.

1. *The capacity to think about one's own thinking.* Thinking is no longer simply an activity; it becomes a process that can itself be examined. It is as if the student can be both a participant in the act of thinking and a spectator watching what goes on.
2. *The capacity to separate thoughts and actions.* In the writing of young children, external action predominates, and the only internal action will be the inclusion of feelings at infrequent points. As students mature, they seem capable of handling two schemes of action—what a character does and what a character thinks. Frequently there is tension between these two schemes; a character may act in a way that is at odds with what he or she is thinking.
3. *The capacity for empathy with adults.* This interest in motives extends to adults who are increasingly seen as more human and less omnipotent than before. They become "understandable."

Bridge to Terabithia   *Bridge to Terabithia* anticipates the intellectual development of the middle-school student. The book concerns a ten-year-old boy, Jess, who feels distant from his own family and disengaged from school.

The one friendship he does make is with an unconventional girl in his class, Leslie. Leslie does not dress like a girl, and Jess discovers—to his embarrassment—that she doesn't act like one when she beats all the fifth-grade boys in a sprint. Together they establish their own private kingdom, Terabithia, in the woods near Leslie's house. At first, the kingdom is Leslie's creation, but as the book develops, Jess is able to participate in the fantasy.

Terabithia is bounded by a ditch that becomes swollen one day during a spring rain. Jess is afraid to use the rope swing to cross, and, to avoid showing his fear, does not meet Leslie to play that day. Instead, he accepts an invitation from his art teacher to visit a gallery. He returns to learn that Leslie, without him, tried to cross the gully, missed the landing, and drowned. In his mourning, Jess grows.

Initially, his most evident growth is in his capacity to deal with adults. His own parents seem distant as does his teacher. To Jess, Leslie's close relationship with her father had been somehow unnatural:

She was learning, she related glowingly at recess, to "understand" her father. It never occurred to Jess that parents were meant to be understood any more than the safe at the Millsburg First National was sitting around begging him to crack it. Parents were what they were; it wasn't up to you to try to puzzle them out. (67)

While there are glimmers that this attitude will change, particularly in his close relationship to his music teacher, the real change occurs when he must deal with Leslie's death. His first reaction is to run. His father goes after him, the first real interaction between father and son in the book. His father gathers him in his arms, and Jess, after an initial struggle, settles into the pick-up truck:

He leaned his weight upon the door of the pick-up and let his head thud-thud against the window. His father drove stiffly without speaking, though once he cleared his throat as though he were going to say something, but he glanced at Jess and closed his mouth.
When they pulled up at the house, his father sat quietly and Jess could feel the man's uncertainty, so he opened the door and got out. (104,106)

We sense the door of the safe being opened, just a crack. While the father doesn't reveal very much, he no longer seems totally incomprehensible to Jess. For the first time in the book, the father is seen as a human being.

But the real breakthrough comes when Jess must go back to

school. He is shocked to see that Leslie's desk has already been removed, and he asks himself why they are in such a hurry to get rid of her. After the pledge of allegiance, the teacher, "Monster Mouth Meyers," asks him to come into the hall with her. There Jess notices that Mrs. Meyers has been crying, and she speaks to him in a softened tone he has not heard before:

"Jesse," she repeated. "I just wanted to give you my sincere sympathy." The words were like a Hallmark card to him, but the tone was new.

He looked up into her face, despite himself. Behind her turned up glasses Mrs. Meyers' narrow eyes were full of tears. For a minute he thought he might cry himself. He and Mrs. Meyers standing in the basement hallway, crying about Leslie Burke. It was so weird he almost laughed instead.

"When my husband died"—Jesse could hardly imagine Mrs. Meyers ever having a husband—"people kept telling me not to cry, kept trying to make me forget." Mrs. Meyers loving, mourning. How could you figure it. "But I didn't want to forget." She took a handkerchief from her sleeve and blew her nose. "This morning when I came in, someone had already taken out her desk." She stopped and blew her nose again. "It—it—we—I never had such a student. In all my years of teaching. I shall always be grateful—"

He wanted to comfort her. He wanted to unsay all the things he ever said about her—even unsay the things Leslie had said. Lord, don't let her find out.

"Yes'm." He couldn't think of anything else to say. (125)

The safe opens.

In this and other exchanges, there is a rich interplay between what Jess sees and what he thinks and what he says. It is almost as if he and the reader are juggling different kinds of awareness. This juggling ability is most apparent in the scene in which Jess visits Leslie's home after her death to join the mourners. He is introduced to Leslie's grandmother, who then breaks down crying and leaves the room. Jess reflects on this incident:

He was glad she was gone. There was something weird about a woman like that crying. It was as if the lady who talked about Polident on TV had suddenly burst into tears. It didn't fit. He looked around the room full of red-eyed adults. Look at me, he wanted to say to them. I'm not crying. A part of him stepped back and examined this thought. (112)

In this short moment we have an observed incident, a reflection on the incident, and finally a reflection upon a reflection. Thought itself becomes a reel that can be wound forward and backward in Jess's mind. Jess is juggling multiple perspectives, multiple worlds, just as throughout the book he has balanced the world of Terabithia and the world on the other side of the gully.

Examples of self-consciousness can be found in a variety of types of student writing, but I will focus on fiction writing. Fiction can assume real importance in the middle-school years because it allows for participating vicariously in experiences without necessarily exposing personal feelings. Students can "tell the truth but tell it slant." I have chosen two stories, one written by a fifth-grader and one written by an eighth-grader. Together they bracket the concept I am discussing. The fifth-grade story shows the emergence of an inner world juxtaposed against an outer one. The eighth-grade story shows near mastery of this technique.

Student Writing

The fifth-grade story, "Serina and Elena," is about two classmates, Serina, the narrator, and Elena, "the meanest, bossiest, smartest person in the fifth grade." Here is the account of the conference the two girls had after they were assigned to team up on a language arts project:

Elena met me in a corner of the room.

"I think we should do our report on Mr. C. W. Carter," Elena said right away. "He's a very interesting guy. He was a millionaire."

I was thinking of a famous poet but I wasn't going to win.

"Okay?" she interrupted, and before I could answer she had gotten out a piece of paper and written, "Mr. C. W. Carter." "Don't just stand there, get over here and help." She said it in such a manner you would have thought our report was due tomorrow. By the end of the class we had taken at least three trips to the library and found out one thing. Mr. C. W. Carter once lived right here in Somerville, California.

"Elena, let's meet at the cemetery at 4:00 to see if we can find Mr. C. W. Carter's grave," I suggested at the end of class.

"I'm not free until 7:00. How about then?" she said.

"I . . . can't," I shuddered. (I was actually a little afraid of going to the graveyard at night.)

In this passage there is a tension between what the narrator does (submit to Elena's suggestions) and what she is thinking (her resentment of Elena and her fear of the cemetery). The scene gains interest because the author has been able to juxtapose the external flow of events with the internal flow of thought.

Most of the story is an account of experiences—the girls are kidnapped, held for ransom, pretend they are dead (significantly, this is Serina's idea), are thrown into the woods, and make it back to safety.

But the writer does not attend solely to the external. After they are thrown into the woods, Serina carries Elena on her back because Elena's foot is swollen. As she is being carried, Elena makes an admission:

"When I was back in the cabin, I realized that I should give other people a chance to speak out and give ideas. I also didn't have a good idea myself."

"Well, Elena, I didn't have to let you always be the boss when I had ideas myself. I was sometimes as guilty of never speaking as you are of always speaking."

In this exchange the writer moves beyond a straight adventure story to one which examines relationships and changes in character. This interest is also evident in the conclusion:

Serina and Elena were able to help the police in apprehending their kidnappers. They also managed to work together to put out an excellent report. However, they never became best friends.

The story could have ended with the next to last line; the external action is concluded before the last sentence. The final sentence closes the internal action of the story.

The other story, "Spring Cleaning," is about a frustrated wealthy woman, Judith Marlon. It begins:

Judith Marlon padded down the ornate staircase in her beach home after she had murdered her only son.

Marlon had set her infant son down near the household cleaners and had opened the Lestoil for him. She leaves a note for the maid and heads on a shopping trip:

Stepping into the garage she smelled the salt air. Why had she killed Ryan, she asked herself. For a number of reasons. She hated motherhood, pregnancy, and everything after that. If she had given birth to a girl it might have been worth it. But she hadn't. Ryan was a truck-loving, loud, bratty, self-centered animal. She pictured him on the bathroom floor; he was probably dead. She giggled as she started the Mercedes and revved the engine a few times.

Everything seems to go according to plans; she comes back to her car after shopping and finds a note from the maid telling her to come to the hospital. There she meets her husband and recites the lines she has carefully rehearsed—"Oh God, Ryan my child. It was all my fault, all my fault." But she learns that Ryan has not died. She steps back from her husband and "everything seemed to slide sideways." A while later, when she wakes up, her husband David is at her bedside:

"Judy, I didn't mean to startle you. You sure did scare me. It's a good thing we were in a hospital when you passed out. What happened?" David's voice irritated her. He was such a puppy.

For a while Judy stares at the ceiling. Then, as the nurse gives her medication she perks up and begins to talk about her spring plans for a new balcony outside her son's room.

Here again, there are two schemes of action—the events of the attempted killing and the thoughts running through Judith Marlon's mind. In fact, the skill of the writer is apparent in her ability to show how appearances do not accurately represent her inner reality. Building the new balcony may appear as an act of consideration but it may be the prelude to another "accident." The author also shows an amazing ability to explore her main character's inner workings, to show the motivation for an almost unexplainable act of cruelty. And while Judith Marlon is not portrayed as a likable character, she does come across as a psychologically plausible one, a woman hemmed in by helpless males.

I am not contending that the stories presented are the work of average students or that they simply happen as part of the natural course of development. But they do show the cutting edge of intelligent storytelling that can be honed by good teaching. This teaching involves asking students to attend to the internal action in stories they read— why do characters act as they do? how do they react? how do they change?

It also involves encouraging students to explore their fictional characters *before* they begin to write. I'm convinced that students rarely know their characters; instead they charge off writing episode after episode filled with stick figures. To move beyond this type of fiction toward what Jack Wilde calls plausibility, it is useful to have students flesh out their characters in much the same way that actors work to understand the roles they are to play. Actors improvise, they place their characters in situations and discover how they would react. Students can mentally improvise by posing questions like the following:

1. What words would I use to describe my main characters?
2. What situations could I create to illustrate these characteristics?
3. What mannerisms do my characters have?
4. What do characters do when they are nervous?
5. Do they have expressions that they use all the time?
6. What are these characters frightened of? most proud of?

Improvisations of this type help students deal with a fundamental problem of fiction writing. When writing about a real, known person, the writer has memories, feelings, and impressions to call upon; the task is to recall and select. The fiction writer must *create* the equivalent of this storehouse, inventing the details and characteristics. Improvisations can help.

Finally, this instruction involves assuming a more enlightened attitude toward adolescent literature than is generally taken. Too often books written for adolescents are treated like mental junk food, maybe a little more stimulating than Saturday morning cartoons, but not by much. Darwin Turner, the director of the NCTE Commission on Literature, has recently bemoaned the fact that adolescent literature is sometimes being substituted for "older (and newer) works of authors with artistic concerns—works that require closer reading." (1984:5)

This statement misses the point. The value of much adolescent literature is not that it promotes close reading, or even that it appeals to students because of its realism. The best of these books celebrate the emerging self-consciousness of the main characters, their ability to monitor their own thoughts and feelings, as well as their ability to penetrate those of others. With this ability comes a sense of independence—of self.

And few books celebrate this personal intelligence better than Katherine Paterson's *Bridge to Terabithia*.

Near the end of *Bridge to Terabithia*, Jess builds a bridge—one which crosses the gully where Leslie died. As expected, his youngest sister, Maybelle, has followed him. She pleads with Jess to let her cross the bridge, promising that she won't tell Joyce Ann, an older sister who has given Jess nothing but trouble throughout the book. But Jess says that maybe, sometime, she can even tell Joyce Ann how to be Queen of Terabithia. For now, though, Maybelle is the new queen, and Jess leads her across:

> And when he finished (the bridge) he put flowers in her hair and led her across the bridge—the great bridge to Terabithia—which might look to someone with no magic like a few planks across a nearly dry gully.
> "Shh," he said. "Look."
> "Where?"
> "Can't you see 'um," he whispered. "All the Terabithians standing on tiptoe to see you."
> "Me?"
> "Shhh, yes. There's a rumor that the beautiful girl arriving today might be the queen they've been waiting for." (128)

Terabithia didn't die with Leslie, but it is now connected to the mainland by a bridge—not the only bridge Jess has built. He has built connections to his family, and to adults who no longer seem as closed as the Millsburg safe. And he has built them within—he is better able to understand his own grief and to appreciate the gift Leslie has given him. These bridges make transit easier. They allow for the movement of thought and affection that would have been impossible earlier.

So what can a writing program do in the middle school? It can help in the building of bridges—by encouraging students to stand back and look at their own thinking, by encouraging them to explore the motivations, perceptions, and feelings of others, by encouraging them to link self and self, acting self and contemplating self. The result will not be a continuation of elementary school, nor will it be a watered-down version of the high school curriculum. It will, instead, capitalize on the emerging power—the self-consciousness—of the adolescent mind.

References

Gardner, Howard. *Frames of Mind.* New York: Basic Books, 1983.
Konigsburg, E. L. *From the Mixed-Up Files of Mrs. Basil E. Frank-weiler.* New York: Dell, 1967.
Paterson, Katherine. *Bridge to Terabithia.* New York: Avon Books, 1978.
Turner, Darwin. Quoted in *Newsletter* of the New England Association of Teachers of English 22 (Fall, 1984).

The student paper "Serina and Elena" was written in Jack Wilde's fifth-grade class at the Bernice Ray School (Hanover, New Hampshire). "Spring Cleaning" was written in David Calloway's eighth-grade class in Lyme (N.H.) Elementary School. I want to express my appreciation to both these fine teachers who have helped me see what middle school students can do.

Play, Power, and Plausibility: The Growth of Fiction Writers

JACK WILDE

Ten minutes later, when Mark and Patrick got to school in their tanks and planes, they saw King Kong. Mark started firing his machine guns. Two of the bombers started bombing. Most of the tanks started firing their guns.

King Kong was just about to step on the school when Mr. Vogel ran up to him and yelled, "Don't step on my school!"

So instead of stepping on the school, King Kong stepped on Mr. Vogel.

—*excerpt from "War with King Kong"*

Charles's story, or a variation of it, is the story that all of us in the classroom have encountered. It challenges the teacher:

—Why are these stories so prevalent?
—What can we as educators learn from these stories?
—How can we build on the interests and abilities shown in these stories?

I picked this excerpt because it is typical and because it shows the reasons for fiction's appeal: power and play. Rarely do we as adults immerse ourselves in the creative power of language, or exhilarate in word play for its own sake. That, however, is exactly what Charles has done. He has rewarded his friends by empowering them with weapons, and created a situation in which Mr. Vogel, the school principal, is taken at his word and suffers the consequences. But the piece has little cohesion and no psychological depth or motive outside of the desire to play and enjoy the results.

This may be the archetype, but we meet other forms of fiction in the classroom; they arise from other sources and incorporate other resources. Charles was ten when he wrote that story; here is a story by Jessica, age six:

Once there was a monkey. The monkey's name was Trouble. The reason his name was Trouble was because he was a lot of trouble.

He got into the medicine cabinet and ate pills that were poison if you didn't have the sickness. So isn't he a lot of trouble? The End.

Jessica wrote that story on her own. It was neither an assignment nor had school time been provided for the work. What had been provided was a strong comprehensible story type that Jessica had heard in *The Stupids*, a series by Harry Allard and James Marshall. Without any formal analysis she abstracted the story's structure.

1. A character is labelled as stupid/troublesome/smart.
2. The character does something to prove that the label is apt.
3. The writer confirms the nature of the character with a rhetorical question.

Jessica produced her own version of "The Stupids." She did it because it was sanctioned; that is, she saw it as a legitimate form because it existed as a trade book and was read by the teacher. Second, she generated the story because she had a structure to hang the story on (see Blackburn's essay in this collection). Mimicry, then, is another driving force for fiction.

A third force generating fiction both in and out of the classroom is the comfort or safety that fiction can provide the writer. I have had children in first grade up through fifth grade who could not write comfortably about themselves. They needed the distance of "pretend" to explore issues that affected their lives.

I spend this much time exploring why children write fiction because it is the overwhelming genre of choice. Several times over the course of the school year, my students are given the opportunity to choose topics and genres. Again and again, more than eighty percent choose fiction. I began to look for ways that capitalized on both the interest and the underlying reasons for the interest. I was also looking for ways to advance their understanding of fiction. In the rest of this chapter, I will discuss an assignment, the results, and a general view of teaching fiction in the classroom.

The Assignment and Its Rationale

My fifth-grade students were asked to write a short story that portrayed a character change in at least one of the main characters. After reading the story the reader must know the following:

Important facets about the character's initial internal state.
The event or events that led to the altered internal state.
The altered internal state.

The other requirement is that the change must be accepted by the reader as plausible.

We automatically compare a work of fiction to reality—physical or psychic—and judge accordingly. The art and craft of fiction, according to John Gardner (1983), is "to make up convincing human beings and create for them situations and actions by means of which they come to know themselves and reveal themselves to the reader" (p. 15). My assignment, then, forced the students to deal with one of the fundamental constraints of fiction—plausibility. They were being asked to work with it in an area where they possessed some experience—character change. Like professional writers, my students had to honor the reader's sense of credibility.

While the issue of plausibility focuses to some extent on the character, the main focus is on the event or events that cause the change to occur—the middle of the story. It is often easier for students to focus on leads and endings. By its very nature, the assignment provides a chance for students to get a sense of the importance of the middle of a story. At the same time, they are given a way of working on the story to make it stronger as they focus on plausibility.

A second important reason for the assignment is the genre option it creates for the writer. Donald Murray (1982) writes about the importance of genre as one of the forms that the call to write can take. As teachers, we have to provide experiences to increase our students' vocabulary of genres.

Finally, but just as importantly, I give the assignment because it is complex. Students must feel that they are progressing and that they are performing tasks which match their mental abilities. Too often, students are stuck on war stories or adventure stories, failing to see other ways to structure their experience and interest. We must provide them with that challenge.

We began working on the assignment months before the students actually knew about it. From the beginning of the school year my students write every day. The writing alternates between being their choice and being an assigned genre or topic. I use the process approach to writing as described by Donald Graves (1983), emphasizing conferences. While the writing and conferences are going on I am also reading to my students every day. The change-of-character story assignment comes in the middle of the year. Several months before the assignment, I start to read fiction that deals with changed internal states (e.g., *Bridge to Terabithia, A Proud Taste for Scarlet and Miniver, The Phantom Tollbooth*). We hold conferences on the books I read aloud to them in the same way that we discuss each other's writings, pointing to the parts we find effective, asking questions for clarification and emphasis, and trying to summarize the author's story. We also keep track of the character's initial and final internal states and analyze the author's way of presenting the story. When we come to

Doing the Assignment

the assignment, they have heard, analyzed, and responded to professional writers' work in the same genre.

However, those models are all book length. So I begin the assignment proper by reading them Ivan Turgenev's "The Quail," a short story about a young boy who wants more than anything to hunt with a gun like his father; a boy who, in the end, because of a specific incident, will never hunt. As before, I read the story and then we talk about it. This time, however, we go on to talk specifically about character change. I ask them about ways that they think they have changed, or that people they know have changed. We then start making lists, individually and collectively, of observed and possible changes. Every year at this point someone asks if the change has to be in a positive direction (e.g., from mean to kind). Discussion always leads to the conclusion that change can go in either direction.

Next, we start making lists of plausible reasons for the occurrence of the change. I always try to push my students to develop long lists (i.e., ten reasons) so that they will stretch themselves, and in so doing, discover ideas and feelings that they didn't know they had. We talk about the reasons for the change together, testing them for plausibility.

At the same time we talk about and work on character description. We look in books to see the different ways that characters are revealed to the reader—through dialogue, anecdote, and action. For example, much of Eleanor of Aquitaine's personality is revealed through dialogue in A Proud Taste of Scarlet and Miniver. We read passages that show character traits; we discuss them; then the children try to show one or two character traits through a dialogue they write themselves. The dialogues are read in class, and the rest of the class tries to guess the traits that the writer hoped to exhibit in the dialogue. After experimenting with different forms of character portrayal, the students choose one, and begin their stories.

Once students begin to write, they begin to confer. Conferences focus on character description, action, and plausibility. In full class meetings, in small group conferences, and in teacher-student conferences we ask:

1. Do I get a clear picture of what this character is like?
2. Does my interpretation of the character match the intention of the author?
3. Do the actions of the characters fit their personalities?
4. How does the character change?
5. Are the events of the story sufficient to cause the change?

Near the beginning of the unit, we hold most of the conferences as a whole class in the last twenty minutes of a writing period. As students become comfortable with this type of questioning, other conference formats are introduced.

Before looking at the results, it is important to make clear what this assignment is not. It is not a story starter, those packaged gimmicks that are supposed to pique a student's interest and cause the creative juices to flow. Nor is the assignment an exercise in what James Moffett (1968) called "decomposition," that is, creating some atomistic writing task like sentence combining, devoid of a larger purpose, with the belief that the sum total of such tasks is the creation of the writer. My assignment neither restricts the student's ability to think nor misrepresents the writing process. Rather, it places certain constraints on the student so that in the end, the student will be freer to organize and write about the world because of an expanded repertoire of writing forms.

As one would imagine, the results of the writing are varied. Very few children have difficulty understanding the assignment. Of the few who end up not writing about a change, most are wedded too closely to a real character or situation, and are unable in the end to fictionalize the story. One girl, for example, tried to change her best friend from a constant classroom clown to a contrite, committed student. She had the girl get in trouble and prepare to change, but in the end, the author wrote that the girl could not change. David and Judy will serve as examples of the range of typical classroom performance.

The Results

David had difficulty writing personal narrative. He would do anything to avoid journal writing or personal storytelling, but he had a keen sense of humor and a willingness to write in any other mode. For this assignment David created a character, Bill Porkorn, who came into a lot of money selling pork. He used the money self-indulgently to go to Hawaii. He then came into some more money when the rest of the pork sold. Bill's reaction: to think of all he could buy—a yacht, a big limo, or a swimming pool. At this point David originally had Bill's friend, Joe, pick up a newspaper. Joe reads Bill a story about the famine in India. Bill immediately decides to give money to Oxfam. When David met with his peers for a group conference, they asked about and reacted to this sudden change in Bill's character without an event of sufficient magnitude to warrant the change. David, with some peer advice, went back and worked on his story. He made the information about the famine reach Bill through television news, feeling that would have more impact. Then at the end of the story David added:

Joe was on Bill's back until Bill donated the money. The large donation was announced on TV. Bill was interviewed many times. Because of this, Bill made many more donations, large and small!!!

Almost as an afterthought, David included a realistic psychological component to Bill's gift-giving. That insight was included because of the focus on plausibility in the change-of-character story.

Judy had done all her preliminary work and had begun to write her story when she approached me at the conference table: "How should I get to the end? I know what's going to happen at the end of my story but I don't want to get there too fast."

"What do you mean?" I asked her.

Judy had decided that her character, Mr. Whitestaff, an elderly loner, would go from being outwardly mean and gruff to being welcoming and accepting. She knew that the pivotal event would be the presentation of a kitten to Mr. Whitestaff by Clara, an eleven-year-old who would by chance come in contact with him. Judy wrestled with the possibility that Whitestaff would change after receiving the gift but decided that was not plausible. This, I learned in conference with her, is what Judy meant when she said that she was getting to the end too fast.

"He couldn't change that fast," Judy stated, looking past me as she spoke. "I know, the girl could come several times, maybe with flowers." She returned to her seat having solved her own problem and continued writing.

Here is Judy's complete story about Mr. Whitestaff and Clara:

One brisk June morning I woke up feeling very radiant. I jumped out of bed with tremendous energy. Summer vacation had just started. I put on my new birthday outfit, brushed and braided my long red hair and finally skipped out of my room. When I entered the kitchen, I saw my Mom. She was in her blue plush robe reading the paper. "Hi Mom," I said.

"Hi Clara," she replied. "What do you want for breakfast?"

"Shredded Wheat but I'll get it." I reached up in the cabinet to get a bowl then to the cabinet to the left to get the Shredded Wheat. I settled down and began eating when all of a sudden the phone rang.

"I'll get it," my Mom screamed. I continued eating. She talked for awhile and then hung up.

"Claaara" she called. "Be a doll and go over to Archibald Whitestaff's and get a package of ours that accidentally came to his house."

"Oh, I don't want to. I hear he's very mean."

"Now, Honey, you'll only be face to face with him a minute."

"Ohhh," I replied.

"Thanks, Hun."

I walked out the door feeling nervous. What if he yells at me? I thought. I walked up a path that leads to a small meadow filled with Goldenrod, Paintbrush, Dandelion, and scentful Clover. Its beauty made me feel confident. I wished I could stay there and dream forever. I lazily walked through the meadow. Finally I came upon a bank. A rabbit lolloped into the distance. I followed a path through some brush and then finally came upon a big old Victorian house surrounded by rose bushes. I went up the walk and knocked on the door. It was a long time before I heard some puttering about in the house. Finally, the big oak door opened. I felt small and scared as I looked at the tall slim figure dressed in a red velvet robe.

"Yes," he said in a very gruff voice.

"I-I I'm here" I said looking into his sad grey eyes, "to get the package that came here by accident."

"Just a minute," he replied and walked back in the house grumbling. I waited a minute until he came back carrying a small box.

"Here," he said handing the box to me.

"Thank you," I said in a small, tight voice. I turned and got halfway down the lawn when Mr. Whitestaff yelled at me.

"Hey you there. Were you the child who broke a twig off my $12.00 rose bush.?"

"N-No Sir. I've never been to your house," I said. "Goodbye." I started across the lawn again when he yelled, "I know who you are—you're the one who knocked the petals off a tulip of mine."

"No Sir, I told you. I've never been to your house before. I'm sorry, I really have to go." I made it to the very edge of the lawn when he yelled, "You're one of those juvenile delinquents who smashed my grass down, aren't you?" This time I didn't even bother to go back. I just yelled, "No, I'm not. I just have to go now or my Mom will worry."

As I walked through the meadow I thought "Dumb ole insane man—I hope aphids eat all his $12.00 rose bushes." I ran all the way home. As I ran into the mud room Mom said, "Whoa! Slow down! What's the matter?"

"Well, nothing really—Um (pause) Why do you think an old man would ask me if I broke a twig off his rose bush and little things like that? He knew I've never been by his house."

"Well, he's old and he lost the one person left in his life and now he's very lonely. Maybe he wanted you to stay but he did not know how to ask you."

"Oh, I see," I said, feeling a little better. "I wish there was something I could do. I mean it's kind of sad."

"Honey, there is something you can do. Be his friend. Talk to him. Let him work his way into your heart," said Mom gently.

"But how?" I questioned.

"Just talk to him."

"OK, I will tomorrow."

The next morning I woke up, pushed away my down comforter, and got out of bed. I put my hair in a pony braid, put on a pretty but plain print dress, and went downstairs. I went into the kitchen and fixed my usual Shredded Wheat. While I was eating my Mom walked in. I quickly finished my last bite and said, "Mom, I would feel weird going to Mr. Whitestaff's for no reason. It's like Hi Mr. Whitestaff. I'm here to let you into my heart." (ha ha)

"Well you mentioned he said something about smashing his buttercup. Get a pot, plant one, and give it to him."

"Oh, that's what I'll do, thanks."

"Yep," she replied.

I walked to the mud room and got a summer coat, then to the greenhouse. I combed through the pile of junk and found a nice pot. I walked out into our tulip patch and dug up a bulb with a nice flower. I got some gardening soil and potted the bulb. I went in and told my Mom where I was going and left. I walked through that pretty meadow and then up the bank. The large house came into sight. I walked up the steps and knocked. In a few seconds that old oak door opened. I got that same feeling, that same small scared feeling as the velvet robed figure appeared.

"Oh, it's you again. Come here to finish off my $12.00 rose bush?"

"Eh? No, I came—well—to give you this" I said, handing him the pot. "It's a—well—a repayment since you think I crushed the petals of a tulip. So here's a tulip."

"Oh great, another something to water, but thanks anyway."

"Yep," I said.

I was just about to turn and leave as he said, "Oh, by the way, you can come to tea. Probably you juveniles would rather play video games than have tea with an old man so I won't be expecting you. I have tea at 10 A.M."

"Bye," I said. "I'll ask my Mom." I walked home feeling good. Well, I thought. I'm making him less mean. I walked into the house and told my Mom what had happened. She was very pleased.

"Do you think I should go?" I asked.

"Of course, Honey and take it seriously."

"Oh, Mom."

That night I slept with content.

The next day I woke up, put on a dainty party dress, put my hair in plaits, and did other morning basics. I ate breakfast and was ready to go.

"Mom, I'm going," I yelled. I walked towards Mr. Whitestaff's being careful not to dirty my dress. I arrived at his house one minute late. He answered the door. Instead of his usual red velvet robe, he was wearing a baggy pair of old man pants, a blue shirt, and a safari jacket.

"You're a minute late but come in anyway," he said.

He led me into a boring formally decorated room. It was furnished with a small couch with a lace cover, an oak drop leaf table, old vases, a marble top table, a dusty oriental rug, and finally a huge bookcase featuring Mark Twain, Charles Dickens, etc., etc.

"This way" he mumbled as he walked into a dining room. As I followed him I felt sorry for him. I tried to imagine him eating all alone at the huge long table three times a day. On a tray by the table was some tea and cookies.

"Sit down here," he said, pointing to a chair.

We both sat down and he passed some tea and cookies. As I was eating I asked him some questions. When was his birthday? How long had he lived here? etc., etc. That seemed to push a button because he started talking, blurting out personal stuff like about his wife dying.

At the last of my cookie I looked at the clock and said, "I better go now."

"Oh, sure," he said a little disappointed. He led me to the door and opened it.

"Goodbye" he said.

"Yep, goodbye and thanks. I had a good time," I said meaning what I said.

During the next few weeks I went to his house a couple of times. Each time he was a teeny tiny bit less gruff and sad. For instance, the first few times I saw him he greeted me with an almost cheerful grin. Still, he had a lot to change.

One night I was awakened by an awful crying type of noise. I walked around the house but it stopped. I was still interested in what it was so I went to the guestroom and looked.

There was my cat, Tabitha, with a litter of newborn kittens.

About seven weeks later, we had given away three kittens. We still had one really cute one left. Anyway, one morning I was eating breakfast and I had a really good idea.

"Mom," I said. "Didn't I tell you Mr. Whitestaff's birthday was July 20th?"

"Yes, Honey, I believe you did."

"Oh good. That's tomorrow. I think I'll give him Tabitha's last kitten."

"Oh, Honey, that's a very good idea." That night I went to bed feeling good.

The next day I got ready and ate breakfast. I got the kitten, put a bow around its neck, and left. I knocked on Mr. Archibald R. Whitestaff's door. He answered,

"Oh, hi. What brings you here, Clara?"

"Happy Birthday" I said as I gave him the kitten.
"Oh thank you," he said as he gave me a hug. "Thank you for everything."
I knew I had a very special friend.

Judy worked on the character in action. She has provided the reader with a believable character and turned him loose on the page to reveal himself to us. Note that she has also been conscious of, and tried to abide by, the constraint of plausibility. Both her conference and the story itself evidence her adherence to the constraint. Specifically, Clara's reaction to Mr. Whitestaff after their first meeting, "I hope that aphids eat your $12.00 rose bushes"; the change in Mr. Whitestaff's attire; the gradual change in his greeting; and the hug at the end, which acknowledges that he probably could not express his feelings in words, all show gradual character change.

Judy likes writing, but writing does not come easily to her. Before this story, Judy had been entertaining and engaging in her writing. With this story she raised her storytelling to an art as she tried to address a truth. David's story is more representative than Judy's of the class's performance: the change is more abrupt and the pivotal event insufficient for the mature reader. Yet, David too came in touch with psychological reality; because of the assignment and the conferences he started thinking about the ways in which people react to events around them.

My goal as a teacher is for my students to know the world in a number of different ways—scientific, factual, artistic, mathematical, poetic—and for them to feel that they can express what they have to say in a number of different ways. Donald Murray stresses the importance of up-welling in individuals as one goes from thought to written word. One important calling for Murray is genre, knowing that your idea can be expressed in a certain way. I want my students to view fiction as a way to say something about what they know; what they know about people in action. I want them to know that they can present that information, not as some abstract concept, but as a network of specific personal relationships. I hope that through the work in fiction, I have provided one more lens for seeing and presenting the world.

It is the teacher's responsibility to suggest the lens at the appropriate time. Children should be allowed to write fiction from the beginning of school. Middle school seems the ideal time to start to work on plausibility in fiction; middle-school children are increasingly aware of the psychological dimension. They are beginning to develop empathy and an understanding that the world is more than it seems. But unguided children may never discover the richness of fiction. I have had few, if any, children write change-of-character stories on their own. It is only when the teacher shows the child an accessible but new way to see the world that the child will start to grapple with that organization. Judy could write good character description before my assignment, but she had not thought about character change as a way to organize and unite her story elements.

Fiction is the logical outgrowth of mimicked storytelling and exercises in play and power, but the outgrowth is not inexorable. Writing can fixate and be continual play. It is our job, at the appropriate time, to raise it to the next level; to incorporate play and power in the service of plausibility as we help children know themselves and their world better by writing stories.

References

Allard, Harry. *The Stupids Die.* Boston: Houghton Mifflin, 1981.

Gardner, John. *The Art of Fiction.* New York: Knopf, 1983.

Graves, Donald H. *Writing: Teachers and Children at Work.* Exeter, N.H. Heinemann Educational Books, 1983.

Juster, Norton. *The Phantom Tollbooth.* New York: Random House, 1961.

Konigsberg, E. L. *A Proud Taste for Scarlet and Miniver.* New York: Atheneum, 1973.

Moffett, James. *A Student-Centered Language Arts Curriculum, Grades K-6: A Handbook for Teachers.* Boston: Houghton Mifflin, 1968.

Murray, Donald M. "Write Before Writing." In *Learning by Teaching.* Montclair, N.J.: Boynton/Cook, 1982.

Paterson, Katherine. *Bridge to Terabithia.* New York: Crowell, 1977.

Turgenev, Ivan. "The Quail." In *Sounds of a Distant Drum,* by Bill Martin, Jr. New York: Holt, Rinehart and Winston, 1967.

14

Why Can't We Live Like the Monarch Butterfly?

LINDA RIEF

Log entry—January 4, 1984:

If this is really what old is all about, I don't want to grow old. I'm not scared of being old. I'm scared of growing out of being young. Why can't we live like the monarch butterflies? They are ugly when they are young. Then when they spread their wings they soar and the world stands and watches this lovely butterfly.

—*Alison*

I designed a unit entitled "Generations" because I want my students to see learning as connected to situations beyond our classroom walls. I want them to listen to, think about, and interact with people outside the classroom about real issues.

Alison, a student in my eighth-grade English class, was responding in her log to what was on her mind. Our earlier reading and writing about relationships between generations were still fresh in her thoughts. What I intended with the unit seemed to be working.

After reading *How Does It Feel to Be Old?* by Norma Farber, aloud to the students, I said, "This book reminds me of the time my grandmother said she had something special in her top bureau drawer to show me. The smell of April Violets powder permeated the room as she took out a pink-flowered satin case. Inside, rolled in tight coils, were two yard-long braids of jet black hair. It stunned me to think the braids had been cut from my grandmother's hair when she was a teenager. I couldn't imagine her as being someone other than my white-haired, soft-spoken, smooth-skinned grandmother. She began to tell me about the beach trips to Manomet in Grampa's Model-T Ford. It was a wonderful afternoon."

I asked my students, "How often do you speak to your grandparents or parents long enough to find out what memories they hold dear? What life was like for them as teenagers? What life is like for them now? How they feel about growing older?"

"Silence.

"How would you find out?" I asked.

"Ask them!" the students replied.

"What kinds of questions would you ask them?"
We brainstormed and came up with all kinds of questions, such as:

What kind of relationship did you have with your parents?
What was expected of you as a member of a family?
What were the latest fads when you were a teenager?
Did friends ever talk you into doing something you thought was
  wrong? How did you feel?
What concerned or worried you the most as a teenager—in your per-
  sonal life? in the world around you?
In what ways is life better now than when you were a young person?
In what ways was life better when you were young?
What does old mean to you? What does young mean to you?
How would you describe "growing old"?
What *don't* you want to happen to you when you get old?
What worries you the most about growing old?
What are you afraid of? What makes you happy?
If you could give any advice to young people, what would it be?

We then talked about interviewing.

Interviewing   Few opportunities exist in schools for students to gather information
from primary sources. Students don't realize that people often give
them more useful information for writing than books or encyclopedias.
Not only is the information more valuable, but the process involved in
using the gathered material is invaluable to students as writers. In order for students to use the information they gather during an interview
for various kinds of writing they must think out their own arrange-
ments of words and synthesize this information with their own
perceptions.

Students need guidelines for conducting an interview. For example:
Ask the right questions, those which seem to be getting the most information, not just yes or no answers. Ask follow-up questions to preliminary information—things you want to know more about, or you
are still wondering about. Use questions that ask how? why? tell me
more about that . . . .

Show the students a good interview with follow-up questions and a
poor interview that elicits little information, only yes or no answers.

Poor Interview:
Did you like school as a teenager?
  No.
What was life like when you were young?
  Not bad. Not good.

What kind of relationship did you have with your family?
   Good.
Did you like your parents?
   Yes.

Good Interviews:

In what ways was life better when you were a teenager than now?
   The world was a better place to live thirty years ago as far as I'm concerned.
In what way?
   If you wanted something you had to work and save for it. But not anymore.
How's that different from now?
   Now, you just hold a plastic card and you can have it. Kids ask and they get. They don't know the value of hard work and don't have any appreciation of what it takes to earn a living.
Whose fault is that?
   I'm not saying it's the kids' fault. It's the fault of the parents and our society.

—Charlie, age seventy

What was school like when you were a teenager?
   Teachers made school humiliating.
What do you mean by "humiliating"?
   Sometimes I got in trouble in school. I skipped school once and had to sit in the corridor all day with a dunce cap on my head.
What else did they do?
   Once I got caught chewing gum and had to put it on the end of my nose all day. They also made bad grades public.
How did they do that?
   By announcing to the whole class what you got or posting your bad grade as an example to others.

—Elaine, age sixty-two

   Like William Zinsser (1980), I advise:

DON'T USE TAPE RECORDERS! Recording is not writing. Equipment can malfunction, it takes hours to transcribe the words, and there is no longer any involvement in the writing process.

BE EXTREMELY OBSERVANT, WITH HAND, HEART AND EYES. Take down as many exact quotes as possible from the person being interviewed to make the story alive. Try to capture the feelings behind the words—

note any sadness, delight, enthusiasm, confusion, etc. Note what people look like—a physical description, especially of their faces—and note what they do as they talk or react to you—fidget, lean forward, wring their hands, whisper, yell, watch you, or look away. For example:

Pieter B. wrote of Charlie, age seventy: *Charlie is a man of average height, with a kind and caring face that seems fatigued from years of hard work. His hands are worn and slightly wrinkled and his face is permanently darkened from long endless days of working under the hot summer sun.*

Becky B. wrote of Elsie: *Elsie, a small, frail, white-haired lady in her mid-seventies, sits sleepily in an overstuffed chair, occasionally dozing off.*

Seth wrote of Charlie, age eighty-nine: *Tall and heavyset, Charlie sits in his room at the nursing home, staring out the window, longing for the family that isn't there. In very good health, except for eyes stricken with cataracts, he enjoys walking, although it is getting increasingly difficult.*

TRANSCRIBE NOTES TO A FINISHED COMPLETE SENTENCE FORMAT. *Try for a balance between what the person is saying in his own words (through selective quotes that show the person) and what you write to explain and connect what the person is saying.*

The students set up interviews with parents and grandparents. We talked about using nursing home patients to interview in place of, or in addition to, a grandparent. I agreed with the students that sometimes the patients are not the most cooperative or easy to talk to, and questions should therefore be asked selectively.

Before the students left for the nursing home, I read the poem, "The Little Boy and the Old Man" from *A Light in the Attic* by Shel Silverstein, because it shows so succinctly how a small child and an old man share similar problems and feelings. Only years separate people.

The Little Boy and the Old Man

Said the little boy, "Sometimes I drop my spoon."
Said the little old man, "I do that too."
The little boy whispered, "I wet my pants."
"I do that too," laughed the little old man.
Said the little boy, "I often cry."
The old man nodded, "So do I."
"But worst of all," said the boy, "it seems
Grown-ups don't pay attention to me."

And he felt the warmth of a wrinkled old hand.
"I know what you mean," said the little old man.

When the students returned from the nursing home, we began reading and writing about the relationship of generations.

In a literate environment (see Atwell's chapter in this volume), reading and writing cannot be separated. I chose books, poems, essays, and short stories as models for the writing I hoped the students could accomplish.

    Reading

    I had three ways of getting at reading, all designed around writing.

Literature I read to the students

I read poems, short stories, or selected sections of books to the class. They simply listened. Sometimes I asked them to share a response or personal reaction to the piece, but only if they chose to share their response. Sometimes I asked them to share a response in their logs.

Literature I read with the students

We read selected stories, poems, or essays together as the various pieces of writing were being drafted. In addition to modeling good literature, I think students learn to read better if they see words as they listen to someone reading.

    Vocabulary work was built into this kind of reading, perhaps in response to parents questioning, "What *are* you doing with vocabulary?" or perhaps because vocabulary in content is far more palatable and worthwhile than through lists of isolated words. However, I'm still not sure my way is the best way, especially after David, bending over a dictionary, told me, "Boy, you sure know how to ruin a good piece of literature!"

    In response to these poems and stories, students drafted, revised, and wrote responses such as the following:

My father said, when I was six years old, that my mother went on a long trip. What I finally found out was, she had run out on us. I still miss her, but I try not to think about it much.

    —Richard, in response to "The Colt" by Wallace Stegner

The poem "Meditation on His Ninety-First Year," by John Haag, puzzled me, for the man accepted death so calmly. How can anyone sit there and wait until it happens. Death scares me, but puzzles me. I wonder how I will accept death? The poem reminds me of my grandmother. Recently my grandmother went to the hospital. She had a stroke. It was hard for me because nobody would tell me her condition and I couldn't go see her because I was sick. She told me later she wasn't sure if she would live or die. She expected to die, but she didn't.

As soon as she got out of the hospital, I rode my bike straight to her house. She told me she had a stroke and thought she might not live. But she said she had too many things to do and lots left to accomplish. Summer was coming and she had to open up the camp. She said she didn't want anyone to miss her when she was gone, so she said, "I decided. I'm not going!"

"Not only that," she said, "but who would take care of Grampa, and the house?"

And I said, "And what would I do without your love and understanding?"

—Steve

Literature the students read on their own

From a recommended list of books, which included a free choice, the students had eight weeks to read two stories, one specifically on the elderly, the other on family relationships. I asked them to relate their immediate response and feelings to the books, to relate the stories to their own experiences, to talk about the main characters and how they changed, and to talk about what they would have done differently if they had written the book.

Lisa B. wrote:

In the story Getting Nowhere *by Constance Greene, I liked the phrase, "The day dragged on like a turtle out for a walk." It describes a boring day excellently. I disliked the phrase, "That's some piece!" I've never heard a reference to a female that's so crude. It's as if she was a new Porsche or something. If I had written this story, I would have put less emphasis on the stepmother and more on the stepson's problems facing reality.*

While we were reading, we were writing.

Writing   All writing in the unit came from the interview as a primary source of information, in bits and pieces, or simply as stimulation, the stirring of memories.

We talked about good writing. The students feel that good writing pulls a reader in, and keeps her reading. It causes some reaction in a reader and the reader can usually identify with the writing. Because middle-school students are still imitating styles, they need *models* of all kinds of good writing of the type or kind they are asked to do.

At middle-school level students need to write more than personal narrative. I asked the students to attempt several kinds of writing: impression, a personality portrait, and an experience, in addition to writing responses to numerous pieces of literature as they wrote.

Impression

I wanted the students to see the impressions left on others by older people and grandparents, especially those in nursing homes. I include the two following pieces of writing because they are good examples of impressions from a teenager's point of view. I read the poem "Old People" by Fay Longshaw to the class. The poem describes old people as neglected "like an unwanted toy put down and then forgotten." Together we read the short story "The Moustache" by Robert Cormier. The story is about a teenage boy who visits his grandmother in a nursing home. He feels guilty because he hasn't seen her in so long. At the nursing home, he discovers she is not just his grandmother, but a real person, with guilt feelings of her own.

> "I sit here these days, Mike," she said, her voice a lullaby, her hand still holding mine, "and I drift and dream. The days are fuzzy sometimes, merging together. Sometimes it's like I'm not here at all but somewhere else altogether. And I always think of you. Those years we had. Not enough years, Mike, not enough ..."
>
> ... "And I think of that terrible night, Mike, that terrible night. Have you ever really forgiven me for that night?"
>
> "Listen ..." I began. I wanted to say: "Nana, this is Mike your grandson, not Mike your husband."
>
> "Sh ... Sh ..." she whispered, placing a finger as long and cold as a candle against my lips. "Don't say anything. I've waited so long for this moment. To be here. With you. I wondered what I would say if suddenly you walked in that door like other people have done. I've thought and thought about it. And I finally made up my mind—I'd ask you to forgive me. I was too proud to ask before."
>
> ... "Nana," I said. I couldn't keep up the pretense any longer, adding one more burden to my load of guilt, leading her on this way, playing a pathetic game of make-believe with an old woman clinging to memories. She didn't seem to hear me.
>
> *(pp. 207–208)*

After reading this passage, I asked the students to close their eyes: What words come to mind about the nursing home? What's the one dominant feeling or impression you had? What stands out still in your mind?

The students drafted, revised and wrote.

The nursing home
was a series of small,
cramped,
cubicles,
which granted one
just barely enough room
to exist within.
In one such cubicle
sat an elder woman
shying from
any outer form
of activity.
"I'm old now. I'm unable to do that anymore,"
was her excuse
for not playing any games,
not taking walks,
not staying to socialize when a room fills,
and many other pleasurable pastimes.
So she sat
silently,
alone,
in front of her window,
looking out
upon a world
of fluttering autumn leaves
framed
against a seemingly never-ending,
bright-blue sky.

—Lisa

I walked into Oceanside Nursing Home feeling very inferior and small. My assigned elder, Ethel, didn't help. Her attitude made me feel obligated to impress her. Her hearing problem and her soft voice only made matters worse.

"Ethel, how long have you been here?" I yelled, so she would hear me.

She mumbled, as though she didn't want to answer at all.

"What?" I yelled, trying to keep the one-sided conversation going. I tried to be polite.

"Too long!" she grunted, and sighed a disgusted "Pffah!"

I thought the whole room of elderly patients and classmates was staring at me. But they were having the same kind of problems.

"Would you like to play a card game?" I suggested.

"I already told you my name—Ethel. Didn't you read my letter?"

"No, no ... would ... you ... like ... to ... play ... a ... card ... game?" I said again, slowly, loudly, and clearly, trying not to show my frustration.

"Okay," she replied.

We played the most unexciting game of "Crazy Eights" I have ever played. I not only made my moves, but I made hers as well. To make her happy I fixed it so that she won every game. At least that put some oomph into the afternoon.

However, the game brought boredom to Ethel. I suspected such when she said, "Is this all you kids do for fun?"

"No," I mumbled. "Would you like to play ..." I began. But I noticed my class was leaving.

"It was really nice to meet you, Ethel." I moved toward her to give her a hug, but she turned the wheelchair so that her back was facing me.

Maybe she's just frustrated at being alone so much. I hope it wasn't me.

—Ben

Personality Portrait

Together we read the personality portrait of "Annie Lane" from the book *don't send me flowers when I'm dead* by Eva J. Salber. I wanted the students to read a good example of writing that revealed a character in several ways through an interview.

ANNIE LANE—71— *"Don't send me flowers when I'm dead. I want them now."*

Annie Lane, tall and sturdy, her fair complexion shielded from the sun by an old-fashioned sunbonnet, works her land and is proud of it. In very good health, except for deafness, she wears a large hearing aid pinned to her dress.

I was next to the baby in my family. I had to work hard—I was a widow woman's child. I was raised to work. We had to dig our living out of the ground. I quit school when I was in the seventh grade and got married ... My husband was a farmer, too, so I went right on helping him with the farm. We both worked hard. A farmer never gets rich but we lived a happy life ...

I was raised to work and I still enjoy it. I'll go on working as long as I'm able. When I'm not able, when I get to that, I hope I'll do a big day's work and lay down at night and go to sleep and not wake up.

I tell people, "Don't send me flowers when I'm dead. I want them now." It wouldn't do me two cents worth of good after I'm dead to put me in my grave and put a pile of flowers on me as big as this house. If you've got a flower you want me to have, give it to me while I'm living.

(pp. 20–21)

We talked about how a writer reveals a character's personality by describing his or her physical appearance, what the person says or does, the person's thoughts or feelings, and the person's effect on other people. I asked the students to try to describe the person they interviewed—a grandparent or the person at the nursing home.

The students drafted, revised and wrote.

Nana is the kind of person who would give you the shirt off her back, but then complain about how cold she is.

—Ann

Marjorie H., age 68: "Old is older than me. It isn't how you feel, it's how you think."

Marjorie sits down, sliding a pillow behind her somewhat disfig-ured back. She lowers her cigarette, takes up her beer, and picks a white hair off her stylish knit sweater. She is back from her job at a dry cleaners, where she does specialty sewing jobs.

The atmosphere is a comfortable one. The room is clean, although small and cluttered. Her well-favored Welsh Terrier wanders about in search of extra attention from her guests. As Marjorie talks, her eyes reflect the light of knowledge, knowledge of things past and present.

I went to Newton schools, which, according to the census, were some of the best. I didn't like them. They were large schools with forty in a class. My graduating class was one of seven hundred. They weren't intimate, and the social life was a small clique ex-cluding most of us.

If I ever had a chance to live my life over though, I would choose to skip my teen years. I was constantly worried about little things like deadlines on homework. I can't remember ever being that happy during those years.

*If I could give any advice to a young person it would be, "Keep
your cool and you'll live longer." I think kids today still worry too
much.*

—Lisa

Experience

I wanted the students to hear how other writers tell of their experiences with grandparents—to realize that what students might think of
as trivial is what is really important in the experience.

  While writing an experience piece, we read together the poem
"Grandfather" by James K. Cazalas, the essay "On Being a Grand-
daughter" by Margaret Mead, and the short story "Good-bye,
Grandma" by Ray Bradbury. In the short story by Bradbury, great-
grandma, at age ninety, has lain down in her bed knowing it is time
to die. Her family tries to tell her it is not the time.

"Grandma! Great-grandma!"
The rumor of what she was doing dropped down the stairwell, hit,
and spread ripples through the rooms, out doors and windows, and
along the street of elms to the edge of the green ravine.
"Here now, here!"
The family surrounded her bed.
"Just let me lie," she whispered.
Her ailment could not be seen in any microscope; it was a mild
but ever-deepening tiredness, a dim weighting of her sparrow body;
sleepy, sleepier, sleepiest.
As for her children and her children's children—it seemed impossi-
ble that with such a simple act, the most leisurely act in the world,
she could cause such apprehension.
"Great-grandma, now listen—what you're doing is no better than
breaking a lease. This house will fall down without you. You must
give us at least a year's notice!"
... "Grandma, who'll shingle the roof next spring?"
Every April for as far back as there were calendars, you thought
you heard woodpeckers tapping the housetop. But no, it was
Great-grandma somehow transported, single, pounding nails, re-
placing shingles, high in the sky!
"Douglas," she whispered, "don't ever let anyone do the shingles
unless it's fun for them."
"Yes'm."
"Look around come April, and say, 'Who'd like to fix the roof?' And
whichever face lights up is the face you want, Douglas. Because
up there on that roof you can see the whole town going toward
the edge of the earth ..."

(pp. 92–93)

We each wrote about an experience with a grandparent or an elderly person in an attempt to show the kind of relationship we have with that person.

Grandma's chubby body slouches over the stove, waving her hands like a magician, trying to get her meat to cook. I watch her, thinking back ...

She's a funny lady, but she lost a lot of her sense of humor when she became sick. I think back to the first time I spent the night here ...

Grandma looked weak. She had just gotten out of the hospital for a kidney ailment. She wasn't peppy and perked up as usual. We played "Kings to the Corner," her favoite card game.

In the middle of the game she sat back. The room was quiet except for the sound of buses and cars passing below. The smell of her apartment was suddenly swept away in a fraction of a second as a breeze blew at the curtains. The moon glistened through my ginger ale.

Grandma sat like that for a couple of minutes. She looked lost. Her expression was blank ... and something ... just looked wrong, out of place. A tear rolled down her cheek. Just the thought of Grandma being sad dampened my spirits.

Her words came out cold and uncaring. "I'm old!" She brought her hands to her face and examined her wrinkled skin. "I've lost the freedom of myself. They want to put me in a nursing home. You—you have qualities, qualities I'll never have again. Use them. You'll only be cheating yourself if you don't."

I didn't understand her then. I was only ten years old. She was sent to a nursing home, but she got better and returned to her apartment. She's helped me through a lot and I know I'd hate to lose her.

Grandma turns from the stove and sits at the table. She gets so wrapped up in the interview, she forgets the meat and it burns. But it doesn't matter. Before I leave, Grandma smiles, gives me a kiss and her eyes glisten. Now I know what she meant.

—Diana
Based on a true incident.

Publication | Publication is important to students. They need to see their own words in print. They become *real* writers.

The students compiled the final drafts of their writing into individual booklets, made a cover, and chose one sentence (a quote of their own) that showed what they thought about the relationship of generations.

The students wrote:

*Older generations have more experience and reverence for life than
   younger generations.*
*The young and the old need love, attention and confidence in
   themselves.*
*If parents don't show love for their children, the children will not
   learn to love.*
Older generations don't want to be a burden on anyone.

Students indicated the three best pieces of writing in their booklets,
which were to be graded and submitted for consideration for publication in the class anthology. Every student had at least one piece of
writing in our magazine—"Generations—A Literary Experience."

Since our publication came out, Joey, who told me in September
that he really didn't like to write and wasn't very good at it, has asked
me if I know of any other publications, other than ours, that might like
to print his piece on his grandmother. Joey's self-confidence has improved so much, he readily admits he enjoys writing and sharing that
writing now. He reads his own pieces over and over, and reads his
peers' writing in the same booklet. Students need to feel not only
pride in their own words, but they need to see good examples of what
other classmates write.

When I handed out the ivory-colored magazines, I watched as the
students marveled at the professional printing, then quickly turned to
the "Index of Writers," ran their fingers down to their names, mouthed
their page and turned to read. I noticed Kristi as she read. I knew
which piece she was reading and my eyes filled with tears—again.

*It was a dreary evening. I decided to go to bed early. As I was fall-
ing asleep, I thought about how sick my grandfather was and how
I hadn't seen him today. Maybe there was a reason I didn't go to
see him. Maybe because he was looking worse each day. The can-
cer was eating away at him. Maybe when I saw him all I thought
about was how awful it would be if he died. Maybe I already
missed all the great times we used to have that we couldn't now.
Maybe . . .*

I remember my mom coming in to shut off the light.

*I tossed all night long. A ringing telephone startled me. I hoped
maybe it was just a dream, but it kept ringing.*

*"Hello," I said with hesitation. I knew it was about my grand-
father. Why else would anyone be calling at one in the morning?*

"Hi Kris," my aunt replied. "Is your mom there?"

*When my mom got off the phone, she looked at me, then at the
ground.*

"Kris, Bampa died."

I went to school the next day, although I really couldn't concentrate on school work. When I got home I gave my mom a hug and started to cry. She looked at me and said, "I have something for you."

She handed me an envelope. "It's from Bampa," she explained. "He wrote you a letter a few months ago and asked your grandmother not to give it to you until after he passed away."

I took the letter into my room and sat on my bed. I opened the letter, reading it slowly, taking in every word.

Kristi,

I guess you always knew how
much I really loved you. You
brought much joy into my life.
You'll always be my little girl ...
...Remember Kristi, I don't want
any tears shed over this.

Kristi

References

Christensen, Jane. *Your Reading—A Booklist for Jr. High and Middle School Students.* Urbana, Ill.: National Council of Teachers of English, 1983.

Cormier, Robert. *Eight Plus One.* New York: Bantam Books, 1982.

dePaola, Tomie. *Nana Upstairs and Nana Downstairs.* New York: G. P. Putnam's Sons, 1973.

Donelson, Kenneth and Nilsen, Alleen. *Literature for Today's Young Adults.* Glenview, Ill.: Scott, Foresman, 1980.

Farber, Norma. *How Does It Feel to Be Old?.* New York: E. P. Dutton, 1979.

Huck, Charlotte S. *Children's Literature in the Elementary School.* New York: Holt, Rinehart and Winston, 1979.

McDonnell, H., Cohen, R., Gage, T. and Madsen, A. *Literature and Life.* Glenview, Ill.: Scott, Foresman, 1979.

Pooley, Robert C. *Counterpoint in Literature.* Glenview, Ill.: Scott, Foresman, 1967.

Salber, Eva J. *don't send me flowers when I'm dead.* Durham, N. C.: Duke University Press, 1983.

Shanks, Ann Zane. *Old Is What You Get: Dialogues on Aging by the Old and Young.* New York: Viking Press, 1976.

Silverstein, Shel. *A Light in the Attic.* New York: Harper and Row, 1981.

Tway, Eileen. *Reading Ladders for Human Relations.* American Council on Education, Washington, D. C.: 1981.

Welch, B., Eller, W. and Gordon, E. *Introduction to Literature.* Lexington, Mass.: Ginn and Company, 1975.

Zinsser, William. *On Writing Well.* New York: Harper and Row, 1980.

15

Writing and Reading from the Inside Out

NANCIE ATWELL

I'm an English teacher, certified to teach grades seven through twelve, and currently teaching grade eight. I go to a party. I'm introduced to a stranger. He says, "What do you do?" I say, "I'm an English teacher." He says, "Oh. Then I guess I'd better watch my grammar."

This conversation occurs often enough—even at faculty parties—for me to realize I'm a stereotype. Like all stereotypes, I'm one I don't like a whole lot. Fueled by red ink, I'm the self-appointed guardian of your language—somebody so obsessed and narrow it's not outside the realm of possibility that I'd critique your sentence constructions at a cocktail party.

I'm the doorman at what Frank Smith (1983) calls "the club." And there's no access to anyone who can't name and define the parts of speech; who doesn't know George Eliot's real name; who won't appreciate the stories and poetry in some publisher's latest version of a literature anthology; who can't name the Roman equivalents of the Greek deities; whose paragraphs don't conform to Warriner's models.

It's like Ken Kesey said: you're either on the bus, or you're off the bus.

For a long time, I was virtually alone inside the bus. Other adults—including most of my elementary school colleagues—were on the outside. They were generalists; I was the expert. English was my field. I read Literature and subscribed to *The New York Review of Books*.

My students were outsiders too—although every year I'd let a few aboard. The gifted ones, right? whom I'd recognize and elevate, loaning them my own books and responding to their writing in private meetings after school.

I reinforced the stereotype. I taught English as a body of knowledge a few would "get." The rest would never "get" it. (These were the ones I'd intimidate at cocktail parties.)

But sometime over the last three years, when I wasn't watching, the bus filled to its limits, and the walls dissolved. The metaphor became irrelevant because suddenly everyone was inside the bus—*inside written language.* I was there; my colleagues and principal were there; all my students were there.

A shorter version of this article appeared in *Language Arts*.

Let me illustrate.

One afternoon last September five things happened within one fifteen minute period that put a serious crimp in my cocktail party stereotype.

Bob Dyer, the principal at my school, put a Bette Lord novel in my mailbox with the note, "I think you and your kids might enjoy this."

Underneath Lord's book was my copy of Francine Du Plessix-Gray's *Lovers and Tyrants*. Susan Stires, our resource room teacher, had returned it with the note, "God, can she write. Thank you for this."

Under Francine was a message from Nancy Tindal, a kindergarten teacher: "Do you have time some afternoon this week to respond to my Open House speech?"

When I went back to my classroom, I found a note on the chalkboard from a former student who'd borrowed a novel the week before: "Hi. I was here but you weren't. I love *Portrait of Jenny*. Who *is* Robert Nathan? Your favorite freshperson, Amanda."

And finally Andy, another freshperson, came by with a copy of an interview with author Douglas Adams that he'd promised me over the summer.

It was only because these things happened one on top of another that I noticed and considered what was going on. These teachers and students and I are in on something together. I'm going to call what I have around me, what we have together, a literate environment. By literate environment I mean a place where people read, write, and talk about reading and writing; where everybody can be student and teacher; where everybody can come inside.

This chapter is about how we teachers can get our classrooms and schools to become literate environments, how we can help everyone approach written language from the perspective of "insider." I'm grateful to Tom Newkirk in his article "Young Writers as Critical Readers" (1982) for that notion of bringing students inside written language, as critics, as enthusiasts, as participants.

It's as participants in the processes of writing and reading that students—and teachers—become insiders. We become participants when we open up our classrooms and establish workshops where students and teachers write, read and talk about writing and reading. I'm going to separate writing and reading for a while and talk about them one at a time, so I can more effectively talk about them together later on. And I'll start with writing, because that's where I started in my own classroom and school, my own literate environment.

Writing Workshop   I teach writing and reading, as two separate courses each day, to three heterogeneous groups of eighth graders. These groups include special education students. All my students write every day. And every day, almost everybody is doing something different. These are some of the things you'd see them doing if you visited writing workshop.

As insiders, these writers have intentions: things they decide they want to use written language to do. They find their own topics and purposes for writing.

Using insiders' jargon, they call their writing a draft. When drafting, they try to get down on the page what they know and think, to see what they know and think.

They read drafts of their writing—to themselves, and aloud to each other and me—in conferences. We listeners tell writers what we hear and don't hear. We ask questions to help writers think about what's on the page. Sometimes we offer, from our own experiences as writers, alternative approaches or solutions. But we can only offer. Writers who are insiders may reject our advice.

As fellow insiders, we applaud when writers find ways to accomplish what they hoped to accomplish—as they shape the content of their writing, making graceful meanings. Sometimes we suffer all the heartaches and headaches of insiders in the process.

All this thinking, writing, and talking take time. Writers in a workshop take all the time they need to make the writing good. And I haven't touched on the most time-consuming and least visible insiders' activity: all the writing that happens in the heads of people who write. Donald Graves calls this planning "offstage rehearsal": "I wrote this poem in my head, lying in bed this morning" or "On our way home, I knew I wanted to write about what had just happened."

Finally, with pieces that are going public, writers clean up. They put their writing in the forms and formats their readers will need. They edit. Their teachers help, talking with them about new skills and rules, always in one context: how to get this piece to read as the writer wants it to. With their own intentions at stake, insiders take rules seriously. They use the rules and conventions; the rules and conventions don't use them. These writers will never be intimidated by English teachers at cocktail parties.

It sounds nice, doesn't it? Well, getting it to happen is one of the hardest things I've ever done.

Up until three years ago, nobody wrote much of anything at my school. Nobody wrote because nobody taught writing. Nobody taught writing because nobody was trained to teach writing.

Then, with the help of my teacher, Dixie Goswami of Middlebury's Bread Loaf School of English, fifteen teachers established our own, home-grown, in-service program. Its goal was a K–8 writing curriculum. To get there, we *together* got inside writing. We became writers and researchers and started looking at how people write, and why, and the conditions in which people get good at writing (Atwell, 1982). The Atkinson Academy reports of Donald Graves, Lucy Calkins, and Susan Sowers (1978–81) were our research models as we looked at ourselves and our students as writers.

In the end, the writing program we'd sought to develop was much bigger than a program. It's become a way of life. Writing workshop is perpetual—day in, year out—like breathing, but sometimes much, much harder. We're constantly gathering ideas for writing, planning, writing, conferring, and seeing our writing get things done for us in our real worlds.

Mary Ellen Giacobbe (1983) provides a helpful summary of the multitude of qualities characterizing a writing process workshop. She brings it down to three: time, conferences, and responsibility.

Writers need time—to think, write, confer, write, read, write, change our minds, and write some more. Writers need regular time that we can count on, so that even when we aren't writing we're anticipating the time we will be. And we need lots of time—to grow, to see what we think, to shape what we know, to get help where and when we need it.

This help comes during conferences. In conferences, we describe or share what we've written. Others read or listen to our voices, tell us what they hear, and help us reflect on our information, style, and intentions.

Discovering our intentions is what responsibility is all about: As a writer, what do I want to do, need to do? Does this piece of writing, as it stands, do what I want it to? If not, how might I change it?

As young writers work with these questions, other writers work with them, some of them teachers. We teachers respect a writer's final say but, along the way, describe the options we've gleaned from our own experiences as writers collaborating with other writers. Mary Ellen Giacobbe calls this "nudging." We nudge by sharing what we know; we acknowledge the writer's ultimate responsibility by accepting it when our nudges are ignored. But next time around, we nudge again.

When we allow time, conferences, and responsibility, we create contexts in which writers write and get good at writing. We expect students to participate in written language as writers do. And their efforts exceed our expectations as they make written language their business. At our school, over ninety percent of our K–8 students specifically identify themselves as writers.

I know these same principles of writing are at work in many schools and classrooms. Occasionally, I'll become really naive and complacent and imagine that we're on the cutting edge of a trend sweeping the nation, that the U.S.A. is one, big, happy busful of insiders. And just as soon as I start feeling smug, something comes along to take the stars out of my eyes. More often than not, the "something" is a realization about my own teaching. My most recent encounter with reality concerns the teaching of reading.

Reading Workshop At my level, junior high, there seem to be two ways a reading course can go: either a skills/drills/basal textbook approach—essentially an extension of elementary programs—or a watered-down lit. crit. approach of the type found in many high school English classes. Until two years ago, my approach to reading was the latter: pass out the anthologies, introduce the vocabulary, lecture about genre or theme, assign the story or parts of the story, give a quiz on comprehension and vocabulary, conduct a whole-class post mortem, and sometimes assign an essay. Students also had two periods each week of sustained silent reading.

A little over two years ago, I began to be aware of the contradictions between my beliefs about writing and my instruction in reading. I confronted a situation Tom Newkirk calls "the writing ghetto"—this one period each day when students climbed aboard the written language bus, sat behind the wheel, and drove. What they and I did as writers in our writing workshop, and what they and I do as readers, had little to do with what went on in the reading course.

A personal digression: what I do as a reader.

As a reader, I usually decide what I'll read. But I get help—recommendations—from my husband and friends, with whom I talk a lot about books, and from reviews. I also draw on my prior experiences as a reader. I like John Updike's novels; chances are, I'm going to like *The Witches of Eastwick*. And I go back to books I've read, reentering and reconsidering the writing.

Sometimes I engage in activities that involve reading and I can't decide what I'll read. For example, the text is required for the course; the application has to be correctly filled out; I want to serve an interesting, edible dinner. But nobody had better do anything so outright silly as give me a vocabulary quiz, a comprehension test, or a chance to respond that's limited to the kinds of questions found in teachers' guides or high school essay tests.

I read a lot, at least a couple of books a week. And I have routines, times I know I'll read and count on reading—before I go to sleep at night; in the morning when Toby, my husband, is in the bath; at the breakfast table on weekend mornings. Some of my reading happens away from books. I think about characters, plot twists, and turns of phrase. I playback lines of poetry. I suddenly see, in something that happens in my real world, what an author was getting at.

Do you see what I'm getting at?

The same elements that characterize writing workshop characterize my behavior as a reader. I exercise *responsibility,* deciding what and why—or at the very least, how—I'll read. I spend regular, frequent *time* reading and thinking about others' writing. I *confer* with other readers, talking about books naturally as an extension of my life as a reader.

And much of this talk takes place between Toby and me at the dining room table, talk about novels, poems, articles, and editorials, and general literary gossip. That dining room table is a literate environment where we analyze, criticize, interpret, compare, link books with our own knowledge and experiences, and go inside written language.

I'm dwelling on my dining room table because it's become the metaphor I use whenever I think or talk about what I want my reading course to be. As my teaching of writing was transformed by my getting inside writing, so my teaching of reading is changing as my students and I get inside others' writing; in short, as we *read writing* just as we *write reading*.

To get my dining room table into my classroom, I started with the issue of time, expanding independent reading to four class periods per week. In addition to having lots of regular time for reading, kids are deciding what books they'll read and at what pace they'll read them: again, issues of responsibility. They mostly read books that tell stories—fiction, autobiographies and biographies—and poetry. I added titles to the classroom paperback library and included collections of my students' writing as we published magazines through the school year.

Last year's eighth graders, including eight special education students, read an average of thirty-five full-length works, from Blume to Brontë to Verne to Vonnegut to Irving—Washington and John.

The remaining issue, of reading conferences, is one I had to work with. I have seventy students for reading. I needed a practical way to initiate and sustain good, rich, dining room table talk with each of them.

In September, each eighth grader received a folder with a sheaf of notebook paper clipped inside and a letter from me that included these instructions:

This folder is a place for you and me to talk about books, reading, authors and writing. You're to write letters to me, and I'll write letters back to you.

In your letters, talk with me about what you've read. Tell me what you thought and felt and why. Tell me what you liked and didn't like and why. Tell me what these books meant to you and said to you. Ask me questions or for help. And write back to me about my ideas, feelings and questions.

The use of letters was inspired by the dialogue journals kept by sixth-grade teacher Leslee Reed and her students (Staton, 1980). I reasoned, why not use writing to extend kids' thinking about books—to go inside others' written language in written conferences? My hunch was that, since writing allows for a kind of reflection not generally possible with speech, our written talk about books would be more

sustained and considered than oral conferences. Another consideration was the possible connections students might make between what
they read and wrote. As a researcher, I wondered if their own writing
and the writing they read would intersect.

Each year, my students and I have written back and forth almost
three thousand pages of letters. For the remainder of this article, I'll
take you inside two of these sets of correspondence, showing how
two eighth graders got thoroughly inside reading and writing through
participating with me and their peers as readers and writers. And,
most remarkable to me, I chose these two because I thought they
were fairly ordinary. As I looked closer, as always happens with research, I discovered how extraordinary they are.

I'll start with Daniel. You probably already know him. He always wears   Daniel
this outfit: blue jeans, duck boots, and a chamois shirt over a T-shirt.
He owns a dirt bike, a .22, and twenty lobster traps. Daniel wants to
be a lobsterman full time when he finishes school.

At the beginning of grade eight, students answered questions about
themselves as readers and writers. Daniel estimated, "I've read maybe
one or two whole novels in my whole life." He'd never bought a book
or borrowed one from the town library, and read one magazine, *Dirt
Bike*. He could name one book he'd enjoyed reading, Beverly Cleary's
Runaway Ralph, and he said his ideal novel would be about motorcycles and races. In answer to the question, "Are you a writer?" Daniel
was one of that ten percent who said no. He also said, "I don't like
what I write. I never like it."

The first week of school I gave Daniel a new novel and told him I
hadn't read it yet but knew that the author, Susan Beth Pfeffer, wrote
well for kids. I invited Daniel inside. He took *About David,* read it, and
at the end of September told me what he thought.

9/30

Dear Miss Atwell,
    About David.
    *I liked it because it made me feil it happend to me. it was one of
the first books I read that I enjoyed. Because I don't read much. I
liked it when they talked about David and the feilings his friend
and family (or lyns parents) felt.*

10/1

Dear Daniel,
    *Do you think you'd read more if you could find more really
good books? Your note about* About David *made me sad. It seems
like you haven't found many books you've enjoyed. There are so*

many novelists who describe people's feelings as well as Pfeffer does.

For example, I think you'd like Tex, *by S. E. Hinton. Have you read it?*

Write back.

Ms. Atwell

Dear Miss Atwell,

I dont think I would read more because I an too bissee. did you ever read About David? *no I have never read this book.*

When I got around to reading *About David*, I wrote to Daniel about Pfeffer's intentions:

10/25

Dear Daniel,

I read About David *on Wednesday. You're right: it's definitely a book about feelings. I couldn't imagine where Pfeffer could possibly go after opening her novel with a suicide/double murder. But the way she slowly develops the aftermath—focusing on the effects of David's actions on the people who are left—just knocked me out. Thanks for recommending it.*

Ms. Atwell

Our correspondence continued. Then, at the end of October, I panicked about grades—about how to evaluate independent reading— and placed myself squarely between Daniel and books. I set a minimum number of novels to be read each grading period. Daniel, who had finished three novels by this time, revolted.

Dear Ms. Atwell,

Why should people get bad grades because they don't like to read or are slow?! In my case I can't find books I like. All the books I've tried to read I dont like but the 3 I read. I am just saying it's not fair!

Daniel

11/3

Dear Daniel,

I won't give bad grades to people who read slowly. If you put in the time and use it well, you'll get a good grade.

I also won't give bad grades to people who don't like to read. It depresses me that people sometimes feel that way, but I won't give someone a bad grade for an opinion different from mine.

I do give bad grades to people who don't read or don't use reading time well. In this class, which is called reading. I'm expecting my students will read.

I know hundreds of good books, as good as the ones you've read this year and liked. Mrs. Fossett does, too.

Ms. A

Daniel responded: "Thanks for explaining the situation. I will see Mrs. Fossett. And find more books. I'm going to the town library with some friends on Friday and I'll look for some books."

I received a quick note the following Monday: "I did not have good luck at the library and I will have to go out of town to find a good set of books."

That Daniel and his friends were going to the town library as a social occasion was one of many first signs that a literate environment was emerging among eighth graders. In fact, through the rest of the school year, Daniel referred to David, Lance, Amanda, Jenny and other kids in the class, and conversations they'd had about particular novels and authors. Another small sign was Daniel's plan—to look for books to buy, to own.

Other signs appeared. In the spring, Daniel started taking books home to read. I asked why. He responded, "I took it home because it was getting interesting and I just, simply, liked it."

In December, I gave Daniel a copy of *Tex,* and he discovered S. E. Hinton. After that he was independent of me as a reader. With a few exceptions we spent the rest of the school year talking about books Daniel discovered. The motivation to find writers he wanted to read was inside him.

12/22

Ms A. I found That Was Then This Is Now and it is a very good book. I put E.T. back. I'll try it after I finish this one. Or I will find one more of S. E. Hinton's books like The Outsiders.

Capt. Daniel Alley

Daniel finished *That Was Then, This Is Now* on January 6 and wanted more Hinton.

Ms. A.

Now I wont have to get that book and read it. Thanks. Do you know any other good books that are by S. E. Hinton? That Was Then This Is Now was a real good book but I wish it could have ended a lot more happy than it did. It was so sad because you could see Bryen loosing his brother or best friend and it changed his hole life from good to bad.

Daniel

Daniel was one of a number of readers who'd begun to suggest revisions in what they read. For example: "I wish Paula Danziger had made the father less like a cartoon character." "This book got good as I got into it, but I think the author should have tried a different lead." "Parts of this book make no sense and the author should change them."

I think this kind of criticism reflects what students were doing as writers, in writing workshop, at the same time they were reading these novels. In writing workshop they analyzed what they wrote for strengths and weaknesses. They went after effects, playing with the sound of their writing. They worked on providing sufficient detail, on recreating reality for their readers. They experimented with technique—different kinds of leads, ways of using dialogue. They shifted focus by deleting and expanding content. And they talked with me and other writers about what they were doing. I think printed texts stopped seeming sacred to these authors: everybody's writing became fair game.

Daniel started the year by writing a series of one or two paragraph business letters—to Honda, Hubba Bubba Bubble Gum Company (he'd found a piece of strawberry in his pack of raspberry) and actresses Loni Anderson and Valerie Bertinelli, among others. He churned these out. I worried that none of this writing meant much to him. I suggested topics and other modes—I nudged. And I waited.

Then, in December, Daniel started a series of long narratives describing the nonfiction adventures of Daniel and his friends Tyler and Gary and their boats, motorcycles, and bicycles. It's my theory that these emerging topics reflected the writing Daniel was reading: stories about boys on their own without adults, loyal to each other, told with humor and occasional lyricism. In December, Daniel was reading S. E. Hinton *and writing* S. E. Hinton. He published all of these stories as photocopies for Tyler and Gary.

This is a one-page excerpt from "Camping," a five-pager and the very first piece in the Daniel-Tyler-Gary series, which he completed the first week in January.

We were on a ledge so we put the tent so it was half on the rock and half on the dirt. We sat back and looked off. We could see out over the harbor about four miles. "I'm hungry. Let's eat," Tyler demanded.

"Not yet. We only have a little food," I said, taking charge.

"I'll starve!" he said sarcastically.

"Let's do something before dark," Gary said.

"Like what?" I said, like there was nothing to do. We sat thinking for a while.

"Let's go for a ride," Tyler suggested.

"Yeah, to Alfred's store to get some cigars!" We grabbed our helmets and took off, down the trail. The lady working at Alfred's knew their parents, so I had to go in!

"Let's not bother with cigars," I pleaded.

"Don't worry about it; it's going to be easy," Tyler said casually.

"Easy for you to say. You're not going in!"

"Don't be a pup! Just go," Gary laughed.

"I'm goin'; I'm goin'! Don't rush me!" I said, as they rushed me. I had on a felt hat, down touching my sunglasses to hide my face. I also had my collar turned up and stood on tiptoe so I looked bigger. I walked in with a piece of paper, like a shopping list. I looked around like I'd never been in before. I asked for William Penn Braves, like I did not know what they were.

"How many?" the lady asked.

"Five please."

When I got outside, I sighed with relief. (I did not tell them, but I was kind of scared.)

In the spring, Daniel started reading a new genre, survival-in-the-wilderness novels. He started with Arthur Roth's *Two for Survival,* about two boys trying to make it out of the woods to civilization after their plane crashes in a snowstorm. At the same time, Daniel started "Trapped," his own first piece of fiction, about two boys trying to make it out of the woods to civilization after their motorcycle fails in a snowstorm. As Daniel put it, *"Two for Survival* is getting to sound like my piece in parts."

Daniel worked on "Trapped" for five weeks, writing it in two parts. He wrote one draft and made only minor revisions on the page. Most of the exploring for this piece went on in Daniel's head. He spent time sitting thinking before almost every word he wrote. He talked a lot about this piece with other writers. He worried about the credibility of Mike, his narrator and main character. He wondered whether he had enough detail "so readers could see it happening," something he'd noted twice in his letters about Hinton's writing. Daniel also consulted a Boy Scout manual to find out about frostbite symptoms and treatment.

I'll share just the conclusion of "Trapped." In the story so far, Chris and Mike, out motorcycling on a springlike day in February, get caught in a snowstorm and pitch camp. When the temperature drops quickly, Chris suffers frostbite, which Mike treats. Mike makes various attempts to get them both rescued. His plan to tie Chris on the motorcycle and bull their way through the snow has just failed:

I felt the cold again as if I were coming out of an invisible shell. What could I do? Darkness had begun, and I felt like falling into a deep sleep. I was so tired I didn't feel the cold, and I felt weak and limp. I untied Chris, which wasn't easy in my condition. I knew now the snow was too deep to travel in. I grabbed his shoulders and slid him off the seat. His foot got caught on the foot peg. I pulled and the bike came flying over and we went down, too. I felt my back hit the snow, and I lay there silently. How long could this last? It was then I remembered my grandfather telling me all those stories about storms that had lasted for five or ten days. This brought the little hope I'd held down to almost nothing.

Suddenly I heard a low, muffled rumble. I sat up and strained to listen. I heard nothing but the rustle of the trees in the wind. After about five minutes, I heard it again, and it hit me like a bolt of lightning: it was the plow truck doing the road!

I stood up and mindlessly ran toward the faint sound. I only made it a few feet before I collapsed in the knee-deep snow. I again frantically tried to run, but felt dead. I looked toward the sound and saw a yellow, flashing tint through the black, frozen night.

It came closer; I could hardly think. I was warmed by the thought of being saved as the headlights came into sight. With my last remaining strength I stumbled toward Chris. I stood towering above him and screamed, "We're saved! We're saved!" There was no reaction.

"Get up, Chris! Someone is here to pick us up." Still he didn't move. I panicked, not knowing what to do. I was really scared now, that the truck would go by and we'd be lost forever. I blindly wobbled about fifty feet in front of the truck ... and it stopped.

Daniel loved "Trapped." His letters to me consistently included his opinions on how authors were concluding their novels; he loved his conclusion. He said, "I wanted to give the feeling of being trapped and then, at the end, just spring the trap and stop the piece there; like, you're *free*."

At the end of the eighth grade Daniel wrote, "I have said all along that to write well you have to like it. Well, I like it. Yes, I am a writer. I learned to write by gradually writing and getting better ... I used to say I wasn't a writer. But I didn't know that even if I'm writing in school, I am still a writer. My best pieces are the ones that sound like a professional writer wrote it."

Over his eighth grade year, Daniel read twelve novels and wrote me thirty-five letters. He used this year to get inside professional writers' prose and to write reading. And he did this because he had time to read and write his choice of books and topics, and chances to talk with other readers and writers about good writing.

The gains students like Daniel made thrilled me. This pleasure was compounded by the equally impressive growth of other students, some of them already dedicated readers at the beginning of eighth grade. Tara, Daniel's classmate, falls into this category.

Tara

In September Tara said, "I love to read because I love to travel, and good books make me feel like I'm living in the story." She regularly bought books and could name half a dozen novels she'd read over the summer. Tara named her favorite books by listing their authors—Judy Blume, Lois Lowry, and Laura Ingalls Wilder. Books she didn't enjoy reading were textbook anthologies: ". . . books like *Thrust* and *To Turn a Stone,* because the stories are boring and because I didn't like the questions after."

During her eighth-grade year, Tara continued to love books. She read fifty-one novels, September to June.

In September, like Daniel, Tara also provided some information about herself as a writer. And she, like Daniel, said, "No—I'm not a writer. A good writer needs a good imagination. That's not me."

Tara did not connect the writing she read and the writing she wrote. Although, unlike Daniel, she loved to read, the stories she read were someone else's domain—someone, somewhere, graced with a good imagination. Staying on the outside of written language, Tara read *reading.* And in writing class I fought with her for months as she accomplished little of her own, convinced she had no imagination and nothing to say. The little she wrote she didn't like: a long, unfocused piece about the first day of school that she abandoned, a couple of letters to the principal about school policies, a report for science class, a narrative about a babysitting experience that consumed pages, came to no point, and was eventually abandoned, too. I lost sleep over Tara.

But in reading class, Tara wrote—pages and pages and pages of letters. She was fascinated with what she did as a reader and how it compared with what I did as a reader.

9/27

When I read, it's a special time for me to be alone. I sit on my bed with a pillow leaning against the wall and another one on my lap so I don't have to hold my arms up. I get completely relaxed. Also, after I finish reading, I just sit for a while thinking about the book. So by the time I see anyone, the feeling is gone. The only thing that bothers me is when I get a phone call or if it's time for dinner and I'm right in the middle of a good book. I try to get the interruption over with so I can get back to reading. How about you?

When you read, do you do it to take your mind off your problems and to go into a different world, or just for pleasure, or both? I think I do it for both.

Also, if you have your mind on a problem and then try to read, do you have to concentrate a little bit in the beginning to set your mind on the book? I'm just wondering because this happens to me.

Someday I'll write about students' reading processes as they describe them. For example, Tara articulates nicely how she plans ("Now I have about six books lined up to read but I think I'll read *A Wrinkle in Time* next") and how she revises; how she reseeks meaning ("I finished *Waiting Games* ... I had to reread the ending a few times before I understood it"; "The ending of *The Outsiders* works so well I feel like starting over and reading it again.")

Tara also wrote and talked a lot about how what she read made her feel. She cried when Paul died in *P.S., I Love You;* when a boy character behaved badly in another novel she wrote, "I don't know any boys like Danny, but if I did I'd want someone to dump him, just to show him how it feels"; she said, "*A Ring of Endless Light* gave me this wonderful feeling inside I just can't explain."

At the end of December Tara and I started talking about what authors were doing to give her those feelings, as in this exchange about L'Engle's *Ring of Endless Light.*

... I think this book is a good example of describing your surroundings and your thoughts and feelings. What I mean is: I can think back to parts of the story and see pictures of what it looked like. It's great to be able to do that! I really love this book! It's one of the best I've ever read!

Tara

12/20

Dear Tara,

I know exactly what you mean. And the feeling you carry with you is a warm one, a contented one, right? I just reread the novel The French Lieutenant's Woman, *and I'm carrying its "feeling" with me today. I suspect I'll go home tonight and re-read its first ending (it has two) as a way to extend the feeling.*

What is it about good writing that allows us to do this; what makes good books have this effect?

NA

12/20

You're right about my feeling—that's what it's like. I sometimes re-read parts of books just like you might do. I think it is because the authors include so many thoughts, feeling and descriptions that we can "lose" ourselves in the books, in the writing.

Tara

From January on, Tara wrote letters about authors as people making decisions—choosing how they'll present information; controlling tone, voice and style; doing specific things to give her her reading feelings. Her new vocabulary and perspective came from two sources: the way I talked with her about boks and the way students and I talked about their writing in writing workshop.

For example, she wrote, "I like *My Darling, My Hamburger.* I like the technique of the letters. I also like the way the boy's feelings are told—in most novels boys are only objects that talk." "In *And You Give Me a Pain, Elaine,* I like the way the author brings everything together. The small episodes are so different—it's almost like the author wrote many short stories and put them together. Yet they all fit. Like a puzzle!"

And of *Where the Red Fern Grows,* Tara said, "I love the descriptive words, the detail, and the way everything ties in. . . . This book shows a new way to begin a piece—going back in time through thoughts. . . . About *Red Fern:* I pictured the boy as Daniel. I don't know why. Maybe because he's that type."

Like Daniel, Tara's major literary influence in eighth grade was S. E. Hinton, who wrote her first novel, *The Outsiders,* at her dining room table when she was fifteen. Tara, too, started modeling her writing on Hinton's. This excerpt is from March.

I loved The Outsiders! *I can't believe Hinton was only 15! It's really interesting the way she asked her friends for help . . . My latest poem ("Sleep") I thought of on the way to Sugarloaf. I planned out just what I wanted to say. In the part where I repeat myself I did that because of* The Outsiders. *The only reason I thought of doing it this way was because of this book.*

I asked Tara if she were noticing herself reading differently, coming at others' writing as someone who's a writer herself. She replied:

What you said about reading like a writer—I never used to do that. Last year I wouldn't have known what you meant. I guess I really do read books differently now. It's interesting because lots of times I don't realize it when I learn things, but this is something I'm aware of.

Once Tara named it, she knew it. From this point on, she refined and refined her theory:

I just realized I'm starting to like books with points: books that make me think, that have meaning. ... One of the best things you've done for me is you've opened books up, almost like dissecting something in science. I think I enjoy them more now that I can understand and appreciate what the authors have done.

For me, writing and reading are starting to combine. The other night my dad and I were talking about me and why I love to read but don't enjoy writing. "I think it's because I can't write the kinds of things I like to read." This was the night before I wrote "Beautiful Mountains."

"Beautiful Mountains," written at the end of March, was the first piece Tara wrote she thought was good. It was a breakthrough for her as a writer.

3/20

Beautiful Mountains

"This is so fun, and it's beautiful!" was all I could think as Justine and I skied down Lower Winter's Way. We were at Sugarloaf, and this was our first run down. Justine was a little ways ahead of me, but I was too involved in making sure I didn't fall to watch her. This entire slope was covered with moguls so I had to pay attention. Every so often we would stop to look around. It really was beautiful! There were mountains all around, and the trees were so weighted down with snow most were bent over. The mountains were bluish with lots of white patches. There were clouds covering the peaks. I had never seen anything that looked like this, so as we skied down, my mind was filled with beautiful pictures.

All of a sudden, Justine's voice interrupted my thoughts. "Tara!" she yelled in a horrified voice. "Look!" My eyes focused on where she was pointing. Two ski patrolmen were dragging a rescue sled about fifteen feet away from us. The only part of the person that we could see was the face. It was a woman; she reminded me of a mannequin. Her eyes were closed, and even though I've never seen a dead person, that is what I think one would look like. She had fair skin, but underneath it was very dark. She looked so cold. She also looked like she was in pain—tensed up, I guess ... dead; that's the best word to describe how she looked.

The sled passed by in a matter of seconds, but it was long enough to get a picture of her fixed in my mind. I looked again at the once-beautiful mountains. All I could see was her. I'll never know if she was dead, but beautiful mountains will never look the same.

Tara's comments about "Beautiful Mountains," her writing, and her reading were the germs of a report she wrote in May. I gave her a nudge, asking if she'd be interested in studying our letters and describing what had happened to her as a reader and writer. She was interested. In her lead, Tara lays claim to the title she'd refused before: writer.

My Thoughts About Reading and Writing (How They Help Each Other to Help Me)

By Tara

I, as a writer, learned to write by reading, writing, listening to other people's writing, and discussing my writing.

The way reading helps me is when I "open up" a book I've read. To do this I sort out the parts I like and don't like and decide why. I notice how the author started, ended, and tied the middle together. Then, I look for good describing words and the way thoughts and feelings are used.

I try to decide whether or not the book is "good." For me a "good" book is one that I enjoy, one that fully takes me into another world, one that is believable, one that I get so caught up in I want to finish it, and one that I can picture in my mind.

When I finish a book, if I can go back and picture different parts, I know the author added many details and descriptions. This is something I try to do with my own writing.

*Madeleine L'Engle's books (*A Wrinkle in Time *and* A Ring of Endless Light*),* Where the Red Fern Grows *by Wilson Rawls, and* Find a Stranger, Say Goodbye *by Lois Lowry are all good examples of this kind of vivid writing.*

Learning to write well also takes a lot of practice. In the two years I've been writing, I've only written one piece I would consider "good." But I've learned from all the mistakes in my other pieces.

I also learn from other people's work. My one "good" piece ("Beautiful Mountains") was written the way it was because of a few, very good stories by other authors.

I kept "Beautiful Mountains" in my head (without much conversation) because of a piece I really liked by Justine Dymond, entitled "A Night in the Life." I made a point with my piece because of The Outsiders *by S. E. Hinton. I added and took out certain details because of other students' stories I've heard that have too many, not enough, or the wrong details.*

Also, when I finish a good book I like to sit and think about it for a few minutes. When I read "Beautiful Mountains" to my class, there was a few-second silence at the end. I could tell people were thinking about it. This is the kind of response I wanted, and it made me feel good about my piece.

My reading log has also been a big help. Talking (writing) has helped me to understand reading and writing much more than I used to.

All these factors, combined as one, have helped me in gaining knowledge about reading and writing. I read and write differently now and, I would say, better.

Conclusion All these factors are combined as one in one place: a literate environment.

I've used various metaphors to characterize this environment. It's Frank Smith's reading and writing club. It's the Merry Pranksters' bus that holds everyone. It's a dining room table with seventy chairs around it.

A literate environment is not a reading and writing program—a monolithic Writing Process featuring prewriting, writing and rewriting, or some other combination of lock-steps. It isn't even teachers and students corresponding about books. In schools, a literate environment is wherever written language is the natural domain of the children and adults who work and play there.

I've described my own attempts at establishing a literate environment, my own particular methods. But it's beyond specific teaching methodologies that Daniel and Tara point me. They—and all the other eighth grade readers and writers—leave me with a fellow feeling I haven't known before as a teacher. Now that I'm off my English teacher pedestal, I want to deepen and extend this feeling the rest of my years in the classroom.

I think my students and I will find our way together. We're partners in this enterprise, all of us moving together *inside* writing and reading.

References Atwell, Nancie, "Class-Based Writing Research: Teachers Learn from Students." *English Journal* 70 (1982): 84–87.

Giacobbe, Mary Ellen, Classroom Presentation at Northeastern University Writing Workshop, Martha's Vineyard, MA: July, 1983.

Graves, Donald, Lucy Calkins and Susan Sowers, Durham, N. H.: Papers and articles initiated at the Writing Process Labortory, University of New Hampshire: 1978–81.

Newkirk, Thomas, "Young Writers as Critical Readers." In *Understanding Writing,* edited by T. Newkirk and N. Atwell. Chelmsford, MA: Northeast Regional Exchange, 1982.

Smith, Frank, "Reading and Writing Club," presented in an address at the Maine Reading Association Conference, Bangor, Maine, October 1983.

Staton, Jana, "Writing and Counseling: Using a Dialogue Journal." *Language Arts* 57 (1980): 514–18.

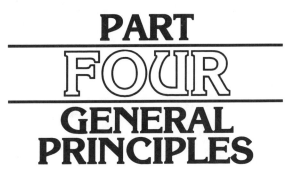

PART FOUR
GENERAL PRINCIPLES

16
Instruction Can Link Reading and Writing

CHARLES CHEW

Common sense suggests some connecting links between reading and writing, yet for at least the last thirty years, reading and writing have not been connected. Reading has dominated the scene in language arts instruction, research, and funding. In most elementary classrooms, reading instruction dominates the day, starts the instructional agenda, controls grouping, and dictates schedules.

Only recently—within the last ten years—has more attention been given to writing. We have learned more in those ten years about what writers do, how writers develop, and how to teach writing than we learned in the previous hundred. Researchers and teachers are beginning to realize that reading and writing are closely linked. I will explore some connections and suggest classroom practices that take advantage of the similarities between reading and writing.

Children who come to school with rich backgrounds in language are more likely to succeed. They will progress with less difficulty in both reading and writing. Many children, however, come to school with fewer language experiences, and they may struggle in our educational system. Nearly every report that has assessed education over the past two years (e.g., *A Nation at Risk*, 1983 and Goodlad, 1984) pointed to the centricity of language in education. Without language facility, children may face failure.

Teachers of children lacking in language experiences have a moral and professional responsibility to expand that experience.

Teachers must talk with children, but even more potent in the development of the language user is the teacher who listens, one who gives attention to the students as they relate experiences, and asks questions that encourage the children to continue to enjoy the experience as they talk. Teachers must foster an environment which recognizes the child's worth as a language user.

Reading and Writing as Extensions of Oral Language

Recent publications in both reading and writing focus on the process. I contend that both processes are similar and complementary. In writing, we talk about prewriting, drafting, revision, and publication. Although we cannot make a one-to-one correlation in the reading pro-

Reading and Writing as Processes

169

cess, I believe the similarities are there and point the way to sound instruction.

Prewriting can involve the student in brainstorming, gathering information, reflection, discussion, to name just a few activities. Is there such a phase in reading? Yes! Sound reading instruction begins before the student reads, and success with the printed page depends on some of the same activities listed above. Instruction can involve students in a discussion of the material to be read before they read it. Students can glean information from headings, highlighted sections, and visual material. Students need to raise questions about what they encounter in the reading experience and predict as they read. Aren't these activities much the same, and shouldn't we expect them to reinforce both learning experiences?

When writers draft, they begin to bring shape to the written piece. Concern focuses on information, purpose, audience, organization, and choice of language. I suggest that the reader deals with the same concepts. What effect does the writer want? What has the author accomplished? Students need experience in recognizing purpose. They should be helped to develop internalized story grammars. They need to understand the "why's" behind language selection.

In revision, the writer brings change to the piece. This change may involve the rearrangement of sentences or paragraphs or the selection of more appropriate vocabulary. Revision, however, could go beyond these changes and involve a major overhaul of the text. During revision, the writer "sees" the piece again and changes it to accomplish the new purpose and effect.

The reader also revises, even though the reader does not physically change what is on the printed page. The reader revises thoughts, predictions, and concepts which pertain to the piece being read. The reader is a mental writer, one who summarizes, gains information, and readjusts. (As readers read they adjust the information base from which they operate and change their predictions of what is yet to come.) Reading research supports this idea that a reader's schemata continually change during the reading experience.

Both reader and writer revise text and meaning during the process. Instructional strategies must show student writers how to look at their work again, how to reread the text with an eye for change if necessary. Student readers need to be shown ways to reevaluate the meaning they derive from the written piece. Readers and writers who can ask questions, can revise what they read and write.

Publication occurs when what is done is shared. Sharing in writing can be the formal presentation of text in a printed manuscript, or it can be as simple as posting a written piece on the bulletin board or placing it in an appropriate spot for readers' eyes. The reader should also share what has been read with someone else. Such sharing can be as simple as a retelling, or a verbal response which in some way permits others to know about the reader's experience and the content of what has been read.

Teachers need to create a classroom atmosphere which fosters sharing. By accepting what is offered by each student, teachers enhance the development, not only of the class as a whole, but of each student as well. Instruction evolves from each student's needs, and these needs become even more defined during publication. Such a classroom not only develops each member's self-concept, but makes each appreciate the skill and experience of every other member of the group.

Instruction in reading and writing should focus on whole pieces of text. Far too often and for too long, students have suffered through a piecemeal, subskill approach to both reading and writing. Research studies and surveys of educational practice confirm that not much time in reading is spent on instruction in comprehension, particularly with longer pieces. Instructional practices in writing echo these findings. National reports indicate that less than 10 percent of a student's time in an English class is spent in writing complete pieces of discourse. Recent reviews of writing texts confirm that most attention is given to drill and practice, while little space is given to the writing process.

Reading and Writing Based on Whole Pieces of Text

Classroom practice, however, can reverse these findings. Teachers can surround children with complete pieces of writing, whole pieces of literature. More time can be given for reading entire books, and sharing can expand experience and interests.

For one thing, teachers must read to children, all children. For young students, books should capitalize on repetition—repetition of words, sentences, parts of the story. These books focus on the rhyme and rhythm of language by accentuating the melody and musicality of language. Books for young children, at times, deliberately play with language. The reading of such books to children helps them to appreciate these characteristics and to use language openly and freely. Children can learn to "say-along" as the teacher reads, to fill in the missing parts of the story, to chime in with the reader when the repetition begins. Children need to be encouraged to tell orally the story they have heard, act out a scene which has been read, or draw a sequence of the story presented by the teacher or another reader.

Teachers of older students also read to them daily. Their students enjoy the stories, become acquainted with books to read, and enjoy banter about what the books mean to them. They live the books with each other and with their teacher.

Whole pieces of text must be the emphasis in both reading and writing.

In both reading and writing, meaning is brought to the text. In writing, this is more obvious because it is the writer who shapes the piece, supplies the details, anticipates the needs of the reader, and attempts to communicate meaning.

The reader, on the other hand, obtains meaning from written discourse and that meaning varies with the experiential background of the reader. Louise Rosenblatt (1978) told us that the reader not only interprets the visual signs but also infuses meaning into them. Readers make meaning and contribute to the text. Frank Smith (1975) tells us the same thing when he says that if there is to be any comprehension, it must come from the meaning the reader brings to the text. Words in and of themselves cannot account for meaning.

Instructionally, teachers can capitalize on this insight by helping students understand how they comprehend when they read, and how as writers they convey what they mean when they write. Students who ask questions about what they write and similarly, about what they read, increase their own understanding of a text. When classmates ask questions, writers realize that their readers do not have the background information an author has. An author cannot assume that all readers will approach what has been written from the same point of view or from the same prior knowledge base. Conferences, particularly as whole-class activities, can help to develop students' awareness of what is needed to clarify, to explicate, to supply detail, and to answer questions of the reader. Conferences indicate to the writer readers' reactions to a written piece.

Instructional practice must consider the relationships among the reader/writer, meaning, and text.

In both reading and writing, errors have meaning. The work of Kenneth Goodman (1970) and Mina Shaughnessy (1977) directs our attention to the fact that mistakes by children may indicate a struggle with new ideas, an attempt to apply old knowledge to new ideas, a new approach to the material, gaps of knowledge and experience, or patterns of the "home" language; and these errors can give us instructional direction. Work in spelling research suggests that mistakes made by young writers may not be mistakes at all, but rather, can be considered part of the children's growth pattern as writers.

Much can be done to capitalize on this error information as students develop as readers and writers. We no longer should stress penalty for the student who errs; rather we need to find ways to make errors steps in development. The speller who makes mistakes needs time and experience to overcome difficulties, but also some direct instruction. Expanded reading experiences and peer sharing also help to eliminate such problems.

Teachers have had a fetish about putting red marks on students' written materials in order to indicate errors. Little aid comes to the student by abundant sprinklings of "sp," "awk," and "¶'s" throughout the written piece. Instead, instruction needs to focus on helping the students themselves become aware of such errors and providing students with strategies to eliminate them from the written product.

Errors of omission of material can be alleviated through peer conferences and by the teacher's response to the written piece. A checklist that asks some direct questions of the writer can help move a child from making repeated errors to a positive learning situation. Drill and practice should have a direct relationship to the errors made in students' own work, rather than a mutantlike approach to skill drill, whether it is needed or not. Positive instruction can take place when instruction relates directly to the work the child has done, whether as a reader or writer.

The separation between reading and writing is long-standing, yet a movement is afoot to bring the two closer together into a more complete approach, which will develop the student as a person competent in reading and writing.

For the benefit of the students in our schools, we need to eliminate the separation between reading and writing, and develop students who are not only readers and writers but who recognize the worth and joy of their reading and writing.

References

Goodlad, John I. *A Place Called School.* New York: McGraw-Hill, 1984.

Goodman, Kenneth S. "Behind the Eye: What Happens in Reading," *Reading: Process and Program.* Urbana, Ill.: National Council of Teachers of English, 1970.

A Nation at Risk: The Imperative for Educational Reform, Report to the Nation and the Secretary of Education by the National Commission on Excellence in Education, April, 1983.

Rosenblatt, Louise M. *The Reader, the Text, the Poem.* Carbondale: Southern Illinois University Press, 1978.

Shaughnessy, Mina. *Errors and Expectations: A Guide for the Teacher of Basic Writing.* New York: Oxford, 1977.

Smith, Frank. *Comprehension and Learning: A Conceptual Framework for Teachers.* New York: Holt, Rinehart and Winston, 1975.

17
Drawing Parallels: Real Writing Real Reading

RUTH HUBBARD

At 11:00 A.M., the children in the sixth-grade class put away their writing folders. It had been a good writing session; the classroom hummed with the activity of a productive studio as students wrote, conferred in small clusters of their own choosing, and shared their writing when they needed an audience. Then, it was reading time. These self-directed writers now awaited Ms. Johnson's instructions.

"*Patterns* group, finish your vocabulary papers. *Reflections* group, do your glossary and reading questions. I'll meet with *Thundering Giants* first."

In marked contrast to the morning's writing session, only two students actually *read* at peak involvement during the ensuing reading time, and the children do not direct their own learning. Ms. Johnson is excited because her students are really writing during daily "writing time," but she is uneasy because these students are *not* really reading during "reading time."

She is enthusiastic about the independence of her students when they write, but uncertain how to transfer this same self-direction to their reading. Teachers who emphasize the process when they teach writing, are changing the philosophy by which they teach reading as well. How do teachers begin to incorporate this shift in philosophy into their teaching?

This question is the focus of a two-year research project at the Mast Way School, a K–5 elementary school in Lee, New Hampshire. Jane Hansen, Donald Graves, Ann Marie Stebbins, and I documented the way the teachers began to teach writing and reading as complementary processes during the 1983–1984 school year. They began by teaching writing as a process, and over the course of this first year, have drawn parallels between these two similar processes of meaning construction, writing and reading.

At Mast Way School, from the first day of school, the teachers set aside time for daily writing. In Pat McLure's first-grade class, for example, the children entered their room at 8:30 and went directly to their writing folders for thirty minutes of writing time. Then, in Pat's and in other classrooms, writing instruction was based on this real writing.

Time

Setting aside time for writing is new, but schools have always planned large blocks of time for reading. Or have they? A recent study of elementary schools found that a very small percentage of time was spent in actual reading (Rosenshine and Berliner, 1978). In typical reading classes, sustained time for really reading books is sacrificed so that myriad reading "skills" can be taught. Bamburger (1976) studied several reading situations in an attempt to discover why some children read and others do not. His study concluded that children read both extensively and well when the main objective was to develop "joy in reading" through time to read real books. Those classes in which teachers concentrated heavily on reading skills did not produce readers who read widely or well. In effect, real reading was trivialized in these skills-oriented classes; students got the message that it was something to do after significant, important work was completed.

Second-grade teacher Leslie Funkhouser wanted to give her class time for reading real books, but wasn't satisfied when she tried Uninterrupted Sustained Silent Reading (USSR). Although her second-graders read every day after lunch in a twenty minute USSR period, their reading instruction was not based on these books. "Mastery Reading" skills sheets still comprised the "prime time" reading. But later in the year, Leslie began to make an effort to model her reading program on her writing class. She told her children they would begin "Reading-like-Writing Time" two days a week. On these days, the children's skills sheets were set aside; instead the children read trade books and stories of their own choice, and held individual and group conferences.

To parallel the instruction to writing time, Leslie began reading class with a quiet reading time, during which she circulated among the students in quick individual conferences. Then each day she would meet with a small group of readers. Just as in writing class, this flexible group was a mix of abilities. Instead of bringing stories they were writing, students brought stories they were reading. Each child read a small section of a book, and other group members made comments and asked questions, while Leslie recorded comments and questions that were asked, and wrote brief notes about the children's reading progress. What about the children not included in these conferences? They knew that during this time, two specific things were expected of them: to continue to read books, and to write an entry in their reading journals every day.

"I'll show you how we do our journals," Johanna explained to visitors one day. "What you do in a journal is you write the date of that day, and then you write down the book, and then you write down the author. Michael is doing a journal now. What he does is, he tells you the information about it, or how he likes it or what he doesn't like about it, or what's funny or sad, or whatever he wants to write about it. And then he puts it in his journal folder.... This is what people do after they do their journal: they keep reading, and they read chapter books or just books they want to read."

When reading time came to a close, the children volunteered to share their reading with the whole class, too, just as they shared their writing. By March, "Reading-like-Writing Time" expanded to a full five-day program. In this classroom, real reading has "prime time."

Pam Bradley, a fourth-grade teacher, was also unhappy that her students' reading time was not well-spent. "I hate teaching reading the way I do." So she did something about it; she put into practice her own version of Atwell's system of responding to students' reading through journals (see Atwell in this collection). In November, Pam and her students began to read trade books during reading time. Comprehension sheets were scrapped in favor of journals the children filled with comments about their own reading. Pam no longer corrected questions from a manual. Instead, she began to write comments and questions in the children's journals and to respond to their individual reading needs, as the following exchange shows:

November 18

Mike: When I start a book that I dislike I probly stop reading the book. What do you do when you start a book and you dislike it?

Mrs. Bradley: I guess I try to read a little more. Sometimes it gets more interesting. If it doesn't, I do not keep reading. There are so many other good books, I look for one.

November 20

Mike: The book that you read to us I thought it was good. I felt that Spinner's dad should of let the fish go because he is so big and Fish should live, too just like you and me. What do you think about the pitcher of "7 A.M. 1948"?

Mrs. B.: The picture reminds me of when my children were all small. I would be up early in the morning, and I'd be alone for a while, but knowing that any second they'd come barreling out of their rooms. It made me miss having little kids in my house.

November 21

Mike: I know what you mean because my aunt misses my two cousens because they're always out playing with their friends and going out on dates with there girl friends. The book that I am read-

ing now is quite bouring to me so I took some of your advice but it still is bouring so I am going to get another book.
How is your book? What is your book about?

Mrs. B.: My book is about a lawyer who is trying to help a boy who is in trouble. I don't know yet if the boy really has broken the law or not. I hope he hasn't. You know, Mike, I love to read. I always have a book in case I have a few minutes of free time.

Pam and her students have time for real reading now, and time for genuine communication about the books they read. "When I corrected comprehension sheets, I just wrote with my arm," Pam Bradley told me in June. "Now, when I respond to the kids' reading in their journals, I write with my head and my heart."

Choice — From an environment that offers time to learn, children can make choices about what they need to support their growing literacy.

—*"Hey, Jean, I know what I'm gonna write about today," Christine confided to her classmate. "My secret hiding place I go to to get away from by brother."*

—*"Did you notice I wrote 'One day' here? That's because it wasn't today, and it wasn't yesterday ... It really was just one day," Jason explained to George and Cheryl as they wrote together.*

—*"I don't want to change it, though," six-year-old Renee told Andy, "and I don't have to, have to, have to."*

Every day, these children learn to make choices in their writing, and they are conscious of their control over these choices—of topic, revision, illustrations. With this control comes commitment to and pride in their work. "Authority over writing belongs to the author," Donald McQuade (1981) states. "To usurp it wastes teachers' time." A successful writing program is based on choice: a successful reading program needs to open the same world of possibilities to children. Just as children who are taught to rely on assigned topics and story starters don't learn to take control of their writing, children who are constantly assigned stories someone else thinks they should read become passive readers (Maehr, 1976; Newkirk, 1982).

Choice of books and stories. Children need to read regularly from books they choose themselves. Pat McLure was confident that her first-graders could handle options and choices in their reading just as they do in their writing. "I'd like all of you to pick a book to read some time during this first working time," she told them. And they showed a range of strategies in the ability to choose appropriate books:

"What I chose was a book I could read that looks interesting," Andy explained to me.

"But how'd you know you could read it?" I asked.

"Well, I read a page. But I really didn't need to, 'cause I've read lots of *Clifford* books and I know they're a cinch."

Jeff chose *The Stunt Man,* by his classmate Nicky. "I chose Nicky's book 'cause he has good illustrations . . . Always!" Jeff told me he knew he could read it ". . . 'cause all of the kids in this class write with words I know. Mostly anyhow."

David returned his first choice. "I didn't choose it any more," he explained. "Look at all the words on this page!" At last he hit on *The Popcorn Book* and contentedly settled down to read.

Leslie Funkhouser's second-graders handled their book choice a little differently. Brian, one of her students, explained to me that they know it's all right to read books of varying difficulty, and that they can identify books as hard or easy. "Well, we have different books we're working on. One could be pretty easy and we can go to it any time. We can choose one that's not too hard, but we need to work on a little more to read it, like there's some words we don't know. Then there's our goal book. That's one we really want to read and it's pretty hard."

Offering children book choices doesn't mean teachers have to throw away basals. Third-grade teacher Jan Roberts began to use the basal more as an anthology of stories, allowing the children choice in the stories and freedom in the discussions. She instructed her students to choose which story they would like to read and discuss. Just as in writing, the groups were based on interest instead of ability and the children ran the discussions themselves. As they read the stories of their choice, they wrote down comments and questions—things that interested them and they wondered about—to bring to their discussions.

Children in other classes too, could choose to read stories from the basals as well as trade books during reading time. There were multiple copies of these books, and the children often wanted to get together to talk about a story they had all read. Some students even monitored their progress by reading stories from increasingly difficult readers, proud of their accomplishment when they mastered a level which was once too hard for them.

Choices in strategy. Book choices are not the only decisions real readers make. In characterizing the act of reading as recreating, Iser (1975) emphasizes this point. "We look forward, we look back, we decide, we change our decisions, we form expectations, we are shocked by their non-fulfillment, we question, we muse, we accept, we reject; this is the dynamic process . . ." (288). Pat McLure helped her students see the decisions they made when they read. "Well, you've all had a chance to look through your books," she began one day as she sat on the carpeted floor with three of her students. "Was anything hard for you?"

Christy shook her head vigorously. "No, I had trouble with this word, but I read the next page and figured it out."

Pat agreed, "That's one good thing you can do when you get stuck reading. Read on and see if you can figure it out."

Andy chimed in, "Pictures can help, too."

"Yes, they can. When you're reading, you use all the clues you can," Pat emphasized.

Later, Pat told me that she was excited that the children discuss the process they use when reading. And she had an explanation. "You know, it's because they're reading independently now and noticing how they're able to read. That independence and freedom is important so they'll continue to forge ahead."

When we make all the choices for our students, we lose the chance to explore new trails to learning with them, and they love the chance to explore. Leslie Funkhouser was surprised when seven-year-old Nathan chose a Beverly Cleary book and continued to read day after day this story far above his reading level. Discussions between the two showed that Nathan both enjoyed and understood this difficult tale.

"How is it that you can understand this book so well?" Leslie asked.

"Well, it's like this," Nathan explained. "I run my eyes down the page and look for conversation. I read that first 'cause it's easier. Then I have sort of an idea of what's happening and I can go back and figure out the other parts even when the words are hard."

Nathan's choice of strategies was an ingenious one, and one that works for him.

Choices in meaning. Readers seeking meaning make choices. In fact, Rosenblatt (1983) contends that "reading consists of a continuous stream of choices on the reader's part" (124). Jan Roberts encourages these options when her third-graders have reading discussions. Jerry, Matt, Denise, and Joan had all read *The Great Houdini* and met to talk about it.

"I think the most important thing about the story was that the teacher cared—really cared—about his student," Jerry began.

Denise shot back, "Nope, I don't think so. I felt more like the teacher is better and wants to prove it."

"I thought the author was reminding us how dangerous the sea is," Joan announced. "And that you have to think about that when you're swimming."

"Yes, that makes sense," Jan Roberts agreed, joining the discussion. "And you may have been tuned in to that because you swim and compete. You know we've talked about how we all bring our personal experiences into our reading."

"I think the author wanted you to know that you can be whatever you want," Matt added.

Jan voiced her opinion, too, but not as teacher-leader; she was not offering her students "the correct" interpretation. "You know, I had a different idea. I thought it was more about learning about Houdini as a person."

Matt smiled, "So yours is the fifth idea."

"Yes."

The discussion continued with divergent interpretations of the story, the teacher offering her viewpoint, but as a "fifth idea." In the past, Jan Roberts' discussions followed the more typical basal pattern. But now, Jan's students have written for several months. They are used to choices and options in their writing and this has implications for the way she teaches reading.

"Last year, I would have pushed and pushed until they came around to my right answer. What a turn around! Now, I'm excited to see their minds going in a million directions. And because I know the kids, I can see that they make interpretations based on their experiences."

Because of the students' freedom to expand and explore rather than focus in on one narrow answer, discussions can take off in unexpected and rewarding directions.

Time passed quickly in Jan's reading class. The children put away their reading folders. It had been a good reading session; the classroom hummed with the activity of a productive studio as students read, conferred in small clusters of their own choosing, and shared their reading when they needed an audience. Jan smiled and echoed my thoughts when she told her class, "Well, folks, I think you're all set."

References

Iser, Wolfgang. *The Implied Reader*. Baltimore: Johns Hopkins Press, 1975.

Maehr, M. L. "Continuing Motivation: An Analysis of a Seldom Considered Outcome," *Review of Educational Research*, vol. 46 (1976): 443–462.

McQuade, Donald. "Creating Communities of Writers." *Journal of Basic Writing* (Summer 1981): 79–89.

Newkirk, Thomas. "Young Writers as Critical Readers." In *Understanding Writing*, T. Newkirk and N. Atwell, eds. Chelmsford, Massachusetts: Northeast Regional Exchange, Inc., 1982.

Rosenblatt, Louise. "The Reading Transaction: What For?" In *Developing Literacy*, R. Parker and F. Davis, eds. Newark, Delaware: IRA, 1983.

Rosenshine, B. V. and Berliner, D. C. "Academic Engaged Time." *British Journal of Teacher Education* 4 (1978): 3–16.

Skills

JANE HANSEN

Much confusion exists about skills instruction within a process-oriented classroom. Whenever I give a talk or conduct a workshop, one of the first questions someone asks me is, "How do you teach skills?" The answer isn't simple.

The skills issue is at the core of the process/product dichotomy. Research on the writing process began because writing teachers emphasized mechanics more than meaning. Reading teachers also receive criticism for too much focus on skills. However, when teachers decide to focus on meaning, they still teach mechanics, because skills help meaning. If writers' skills are poor, readers will have a hard time constructing a message. Similarly, if readers' skills are shaky, those readers will have trouble. So, process teachers do teach skills.

Before I show how teachers teach skills I will give three principles they keep in mind when they work with their students on skills.

1. They teach autonomy. Their students learn not to rely on the teacher but rather, to become independent learners. The teachers structure their classrooms so the students can get help when they need it. The students learn when to ask for help and from whom to make their request.
2. They teach what the students need. These teachers spend time with their students when the students are in the process of reading and writing. They listen while the students try to solve their problems. Then, based upon what they see and hear a student try to do, they teach a skill the student can handle and needs in order to move ahead.
3. They make good use of their time. They may have thirty students and maybe a list of ninety skills to teach. That's twenty-seven hundred encounters. Impossible. When a student needs help, the teacher selects the skill most crucial to the text at hand, but she doesn't teach the skill to only one child. Others take part. However, if there is another child who already knows the skill the writer needs, that child teaches. Several children teach and learn a skill on any one day. The teacher teaches the skills the other children in the classroom can't teach.

There is no standard list of skills to teach for either reading or writing, but many teachers have either their own mental lists, the list in the basal reader or language arts text, the school's curriculum guide, or an accountability system. Regardless, skills are a necessary part of any program. Of the many skills on various lists, I will address study skills, usage, punctuation, phonics, spelling, and context. My main goal is to show ways process-oriented teachers teach skills.

Context Clues   Two kindergarten children sit on a pillow in the classroom library and look at *The Very Hungry Caterpillar* by Eric Carle, the book their teacher had read to them after recess. Other children work on various kinds of activities around the room and their teacher makes her rounds. As she approaches the library, Anna announces, "We can read this!" Their teacher, who has read the book to the class at least five times, responds, "Will you read some to me?"

As they start to read, two nearby children come to listen. Before long, the readers get stuck on the word *after*. Anna, one of the listeners, helps, "Just keep going. You'll get it."

The readers read on, "'(and) _____ that he felt much better.'" One of the readers exclaims, "I know what that part is," and goes back and reads, "'and after that he felt much better.'"

After two more sentences, the teacher continues her rounds, but before she leaves she has a skills conference. "You really like that book, don't you. Why?"

"The food makes me hungry."

"Me too. I noticed back here (teacher points to *after*) you didn't know this word at first. Tell me how you figured it out."

"I think you helped us that way one time. Anna helped."

"Yes, she told you to read ahead and that worked."

The ability to use context clues is the most helpful reading skill. In general, readers use context clues to figure out words more than anything else. Readers who are writers are used to pursuing onward. When they write, they put down their message as it comes and move ahead. They have something in mind and they want to get it down. They don't just string out words. They know words follow words for a reason.

Writers attack reading in a similar fashion if we keep the focus on meaning (Galda, 1984). Young children need many familiar books to read so they can try to construct the meaning themselves. They begin to read the way they begin to write. They jump in fearlessly. Older children also need to use context skills as their first line of attack when they meet an unknown word.

Spelling   Writers don't often produce final products the first time they try a piece of writing. They struggle through their message from beginning to end in order to find out what information they have to work with. Then, they go back and work on smaller and smaller chunks until they get down to the one-word level.

If writers think they should spell correctly on early drafts, they interfere with the main goal of their own writing: produce an interesting message. The following two examples illustrate the difference between how Scott wrote about his grandma and, in contrast, what he may have written if he worried about spelling on his first draft.

Won da me and my fathr and mothr want to my grandmas to viset hr becus she jest cam awt ov the hospdl. She had a ne operashun becus hr ne crdlig is bad. Wal we wr thar we toct with ech othr my gramu told us thot hr ne is betr

Me and my dad and mom saw my grandma. She had a bad leg. It is good now.

Writing teachers judge the first sample as the better piece of writing and, because they want their students to compose interesting material, they do not tell their students to spell correctly on their first drafts. Students who worry about spelling too early tend to use familiar words and compose dull pieces of writing. (For information on invented spelling, see Temple, Nathan, & Burris, 1982.)

Further, if they think the spelling in every piece of writing must be corrected, they interfere with their own progress because the time they spend fixing the spelling on a deadend piece of writing would be better spent on a piece of writing that may turn out to be significant. It is important for writers to write, and writing is composing. The writing teacher wants her students to spend a significant portion of their writing time composing. When they are composing—putting words together—they are practicing their writing and spelling.

However, when a writer decides to bring a piece of writing to final copy, it's time to think about spelling. Whenever possible, the child solves his own problems on his road to becoming an independent learner so he is in charge of his misspelled text.

He circles each word he thinks is spelled incorrectly. Then he finds out how to spell those words. He uses any method other than the teacher. Next, the child goes to a peer and the peer draws other circles if he wonders about the spelling of any words. The writer now checks those words.

At this time, the writer is ready to go to the teacher, who checks the spelling list in the writer's folder to see if he has attended to the words he misspelled on previous texts. Then the teacher goes through the entire text as quickly as possible. If she finds misspellings, she indicates them with a general mark such as, "There's a word for you to check somewhere in these two lines." She does this with maybe two words and corrects the rest herself. The child adds a couple of words to his spelling list. He chooses the words in consultation with the teacher and now, finally, the teacher may teach a skill.

Christy has added *with* and *they* to her list. There is not a skill to teach for the sight word *they* but a lesson can come from *with*. The teacher teaches *with* in whichever way makes sense to the child. Christy may have written *with* as *yith* or *with* as *weth* or *with* as *wif*. In Christy's case, she spelled *with* as *wif*. Her teacher recently heard her read *with* with a *th* so she thinks Christy can learn to spell *with* with a *th* instead of an *f*. In three minutes her teacher dictates *bath, moth* and *path*. As Christy writes each word, the three other children at the table (teach skills lessons with other children present) may choose to write them also.

This lesson is not a test situation. With each word, everyone talks about how to spell it, helps one another spell it right, and comments on the *th* sound.

Christy goes off to find the two or three misspelled words in the sections her teacher marked, and then she will check for punctuation.

Her teacher goes to another section of the room to help someone else at a different cluster of desks.

Eric asks her, "How do you spell *lean*?" Eric is just learning how to listen for sound-symbol correspondences and, therefore, needs to spell his own words. If someone tells him how to spell a word, he won't have to learn phonics. So, when Eric asks how to spell *lean,* his teacher answers, "What do you mean?"

"I lean over when I jump."

"Oh, yes, you do, don't you? Say *lean*."

"*Lean*."

"Yes. Say it again and listen to the way it starts."

"*Lean. /l-l-l/ L*?"

"How do you make an *L*?"

Eric doesn't respond.

The teacher asks, "Who could help you?"

"Denise."

Eric is right in the middle of composing, but he goes to Denise. Young children often demand help with spelling while they are composing initial drafts because their command of phonics is so limited they can't even get their ideas down. They get help from others when they need it.

Phonics   Phonics competence varies from the limited knowledge of novices immersed in invented spelling, to that of more advanced readers like Johanna, who sits in her second-grade classroom in April. She is reading a Shel Silverstein poem and stops at the word *thigh*. She knows it's a body part because it's part of a series of other body parts, but she can't even guess what it might be. Because context won't work (Petty, Petty & Becking, 1984) her teacher waits for Johanna to tackle the word phonetically. Her teacher must hear how Johanna will attack the word in order to know how to help. Johanna finally begins, *t*. Johanna pauses and tries again, *t*.

Her teacher writes *thigh*—/t/ in her notes. She thinks she remembers a *th* problem on a recent day with Johanna, so she glances up her page of notes. Yes, she labeled "Thursday: Tuesday" and also, she said, "t . . . t," when she came to *thistle* in one of her books.

Johanna wants to read the Shel Silverstein poem and looks to her teacher, who says, "Please get your math book." With Johanna's math book in front of them, her teacher continues, "Find three words that have the letters *th*."

Johanna instantly spots *math* and says, "Oh, it's /th/. It starts with /th/."

"Yes. Find two more examples, Johanna."

In a couple more minutes they go back to the poem, and Johanna can label her thigh for the first time, "A *thigh*? What a weird word."

They laugh together and Johanna reads the poem.

The situation might have been different. Johanna might have said /th/, when she saw *thigh*. She might have paused and said /th/ again. This time her teacher could teach the sound for *igh*. A nearby child could jump in, "It looks like *high*." A second child, "And it's in *night*." A third child, "It's *thigh*. I should know. Mine are stiff from hiking yesterday."

The children have found patterns many times, and the teacher watches as they spontaneously start a list of *igh* words.

The teacher leaves them and looks for another child who needs her.

This time the teacher stops at Joshua. He is polishing a piece about getting ready for a football game.

Punctuation

Going to a Football Game

*One dull Sunday morning I got
up & went to the breakfast
table. Mom Pop & my little sister
Jessica were already therre.
Good morning I said. Good morning my father said back. How
would you like to go to a
Foot Ball game? Would I? I
said I'd love too. What time
should we leave? About 2:00*

what will give us unough
time to get ready. I had never
been to a Foot Ball game
before!

Part II

It was almost 2:00. I
can't wait I cant wait.
I kept on saying. My
Dad said he had some good
news & he had some bad news.
I want to hear the good
news first I said. O.K. . . .

Joshua puts boxes around the places he thinks need different punctuation. A friend also checks the punctuation. His teacher begins the
conference by looking at Joshua's list of "Things I Can Do" in his
folder.

Things I Can Do

1. I put capital letters on names of towns
2. I put capital letters on names of teams.
3. I put capital letters on names of people.
4. I put periods after Mr. and Mrs.
5. I put a period at the end of a story.
6. I put a dash in a score like 23–26.

She scans Joshua's work and finds he has attended to these skills.

Then she studies the boxes Joshua has made on his paper. Three
of his boxes follow quotes because he thinks he needed commas at
those places. He has no quotation marks. "Yes, Joshua, you did
pause here when you read. Also, this is where your Dad talked. What
did he say?"

Joshua moves his finger back up the page and reads, "How would
you like to go to a football game?"

His teacher explains, "You need to put quotation marks around his
words. Let's find some in your book."

Joshua opens *Nate the Great,* they find quotation marks, he inserts
them and finds another spot in his writing where someone talks.

His teacher comments, "Yes, now it's clearer to me because I can
see exactly what your dad said."

He goes off to find the rest of the places where he needs quotation marks. (For an interesting, funny essay on punctuation, see Thomas, 1979.)

His teacher goes to another set of desks.

Now we are in a fifth grade classroom, and Marcel has decided to publish his piece about when the police stopped him on his dirt bike. He thinks it is flawless. No edits necessary.

Usage

His teacher begins by checking through Marcel's "Things I Can Do" list.

Things I Can Do

1. I capitalize names, towns, and states.
2. I put periods after abbreviations.
3. I use 'were' with plurals.
4. I use commas inside quotation marks.

She notices that Marcel has forgotten a comma inside one set of quotation marks and says, "You and David found almost everything, but check number four again."

Marcel finds the spot, inserts a comma, and his teacher begins a careful edit. The decision about whether a usage pattern should be corrected is often difficult because usage in writing often reflects oral language patterns. We cannot expect a child to write several usage patterns he does not use when he talks (Fisher, 1980). A child cannot imitate adult language patterns he does not yet use and the confidence of bigger children is shaken if their writing is overcorrected. For young children, if usage is corrected with too much precision, they can't read the corrected piece. Marcel's teacher notes only one usage error and thinks a correction would be appropriate for Marcel. "Me and my friend went to the sand dunes."

They open Marcel's C. S. Lewis book and look for three similar constructions. This takes two minutes and two of Marcel's nearby friends help.

Marcel records "My friend and I" on his list of "Things I Can Do," dates the entry, corrects the phrase in his writing, and chooses to re-write the entire story himself rather than have a typist type it for publication.

Sam approaches his teacher. He is reading a book about some boys on an adventure and found a section where the boys watched some otters. He didn't know for sure what an otter was and there was no picture. Ms. Harrold started to tell Sam about the otters at her cabin

Study Skills

but bit her tongue. She'd better let Sam try on his own first. Then she'd add her tale. "How can you find out, Sam?"

Without an answer, Sam was off to the library where he cornered the librarian. "Ms. Taft, help me find out about otters."

Wise Ms. Taft calmly responded, "What are two places you could look, Sam?"

Sam stopped short. He liked film loops; maybe he could find one on otters. If not, he could always look in an encyclopedia.

The adults return Sam's question to him because they want him to be able to say at the end, "I did it myself." They help him find options when he has a question, but he chooses the process he will use to find his own answer to his own question.

Sam does not find a film loop. He finds a picture in an encyclopedia that he shares with both Ms. Taft and an older boy from another class who happened to be in the library. This boy wondered if otters were like beavers because he had written a report on beavers. They both disappeared around the stacks to find a book about animals. The older boy helped Sam read two paragraphs in a section about otters, "Otters have webbed feet like ducks." Sam decided instantly he had to read this to his class.

He practiced and practiced these two paragraphs and showed off his study skills two days later when he read to his class. They talked about otters. Ms. Harrold related her story about the otters who slide on the icy riverbanks at her cabin in the wintertime. Finally, one of the students asked Sam, "How did you find those paragraphs?"

"Well, Mark's big brother was in the library and showed me this, the index. Here (pause while Sam flips pages) is the word otter and three page numbers. Sometime when you need some information, I'll show you how it works."

Ms. Harrold dated "Knows how to use an index" on Sam's skills list. She also wrote, "Otters. Learned from older student in library. Will teach 'Index' to others."

This cycle goes on. The children need help and their teachers help them become independent. Their teachers give specific assistance in situations when the children can't move ahead. They all remember to attend to mechanics only when these enhance a meaningful, interesting text. The students learn to think about skills as they read and write.

References

Fisher, Carol. "Grammar in the language arts program." In Gay Su Pinnell (Ed.), *Discovering language with children*. Urbana, Illinois: National Council of Teachers of English, 1980.

Galda, Lee. "The Relations between Reading and Writing in Young Children." In *New Directions in Composition Research,* ed. Richard Beach and Lillian S. Bridwell, New York: Guilford Press, 1984.

Petty, Walter T., Petty, Dorothy C., and Becking, Marjorie F., eds. *Experiences in Language: Tools and Techniques for Language Arts Methods*. 4th ed. Boston: Allyn and Bacon, 1984.

Temple, C., Nathan, R., and Burris, N. *The Beginnings of Writing*. Boston: Allyn and Bacon, 1982.

Thomas, Lewis. *The Medusa and the Snail*. New York: Viking Press, 1979.

The Reader's Audience

DONALD GRAVES

Children write for audiences. This isn't news. Writers' texts have to be understood by other people. Children work hard to fashion a piece that will be clear to themselves as first audience as well as to teachers and classmates. They struggle to refine a text, and teachers and other children help them all the way from choosing topics to final copy.

Children also compose texts for audiences when they read. That *is* news. But most readers compose one draft for one audience, the teacher, and teachers often ignore children's need to reread to clarify meaning. Worse, they red-line children's first oral attempts to come up with a good understanding of a text, discouraging future efforts to rework meaning. Still more discouraging is the teacher's lack of provision for broader and more challenging audiences for children's reading in the classroom.

Recent work in writing process research sheds light on children's changing perceptions of audience and the role others play in fostering better writing. Some of these writing data can help us rethink some of our approaches to reading. The data particularly help us rethink the audience role as it contributes to children's understanding and enjoyment of reading. First, I will give a brief review of audience and children's writing, then look more systematically at notions of audience in reading.

Audiences and Writing

Writing is a highly social act in writing process classrooms. Teachers help children from the time they choose a topic through to final copy. They also provide a variety of audiences for their texts. These teachers work hard to help the writer sound like himself as he gains confidence in speaking forcefully and accurately through his material. This is not an easy task, especially if the writer has had many years of schooling in which he has learned not to trust his own voice but only the one that sounds like the teacher. These writers often label any kind of audience as "the enemy." When writers sound like themselves they take more ownership and responsibility for their writing, thinking about writing, future topics, and even their audiences when they are not actually writing.

A rough sense of the sequential development of children's understanding of audience emerges. Our data show that children generally ignore audiences at first, then gradually include them, then take them too much into consideration, and finally get back to a balance between their own voices and their audiences.

In the period when children first ignore classroom audiences, they write for themselves. Their composing behaviors are similar to play activity; they are simply "lost" in reexperiencing events, or in imaginings. They do not separate themselves from the actual process of composing. Later, as children take on concepts of audience in composing, they develop what Donald Murray speaks of as "the other self." They become aware of themselves as first audience, "What do I mean here? What's a better word?" It is specifically through audience response that "the other self," the first voice, the conscious experimenting self, is developed.

Teachers who provide a predictable classroom, as well as carefully structured conferences so that children know how to respond to each other's work without hurting, foster greater risk-taking by young writers. This does not mean that writers get totally predictable questions. Rather, the structure of the conference—receiving and questioning, following one on the other—provides a better framework for a more creative, spontaneous conference. Creativity follows discipline or structure.

Reading and Audiences

For too long we have ignored the fact that children produce texts when they read. Each child brings a different reading history, world, semantic and syntactic knowledge, as well as a different reason for even reading the text at hand. Thus, children are bound to compose different texts when they read. Research at the Center for the Study of Reading at the University of Illinois over the last five years particularly accentuates the importance of individual texts. Unfortunately, most reading textbook manuals cannot accommodate the enormous variance in child texts. Teacher manuals for writing textbooks have the same problem. The textbook has not yet been written (nor can it be) that will predict what children will first say, or how a teacher can fully respond.

Most teaching of reading ignores the composing nature of the reading process. Furthermore, it also ignores the rich possibilities for young readers that developing different texts together allows. Too much reading teaching ignores the power of multiple audiences, both for enjoyment and for developing skill in reading. There are far more occasions for the participation of audiences in a child's reading than we have considered in the past.

Just recently I had the discrepancy in treating written and read texts brought home to me in my own backyard in New Hampshire. I was asked to conduct a teacher workshop on reading and writing in the middle of a very successful writing process program. Two weeks into the program, the teachers were already demonstrating their ability to listen to each other's texts through successive drafts as well as to provide suggestions for improving their colleagues' pieces.

I decided to ask the group to read X. J. Kennedy's poem, "Little Elegy," write about it, wrestle with how they thought the poem ought to be read aloud, and then share their decision by reading aloud to two other participants.

Little Elegy

(for a child who skipped rope)

Here lies resting, out of breath,
Out of turns, Elizabeth
Whose quicksilver toes not quite
Cleared the whirring edge of night.

Earth whose circles round us skim,
Till they catch the lightest limb,
Shelter now Elizabeth
And for her sake trip up Death.

A few minutes into the small group sharing it was clear that conflict was everywhere. Some people moved away from the chairs of friends, and dark clouds overshadowed heretofore eager faces. Listening stopped. Emergent texts were treated as final texts. The notion that listening was part of working with a printed text by a third author went out the window. Here we were, ninety professionals in a workshop, with ninety interpretations of the text. That is the expected, the natural outcome of any reading event of this type. Consistent with current practice, we red-line the first drafts of our colleagues' new texts in reading, while carefully listening to their texts in writing.

It is only natural that the data from writing creep in to help us reexamine the nature of audience and reading. Right now we are at the point of discussing the anatomy of audience and reading. We are still discovering components, many of them influenced by data from writing. Physiology, or the dynamics and development of a sense of audience in reading, is yet to come. A look at audience components, some hypotheses about their functioning, and their implications for the teaching of reading follow. Some of these preliminary data on reading have also affected our notions about the teaching of writing.

Reading and
Audience

The Many Faces of Audience

As in writing, two major classifications emerge: the reader herself, and then all others, depending on how the text is shared. The other self carries several selves that participate in the creation of a text: the historical self, the problem-solving self, and the reader's dialogue with the original author of the piece. The external audience is made up of the teacher, the group in which interpretations of texts are governed, and the audience actually *chosen* by the reader of the piece.

Other Self

The other self is multifaceted. As I read a text I am often (with problem texts) very conscious of my history as a reader, my technical approach to the subject, as well as what I want to take away for myself. As I make my way into a reading, it is often several paragraphs or even pages before I have created enough of a text for my own reading voice to begin to work with the original author of the piece, or with that other part of me that is making sense of what is there, or of what use I will make of the text. Sometimes I have to stop, reread, then plunge ahead again, depending on the demands of the information and the uses I will make of it.

A large part of my reading is just for me. I read detective stories, or Russian novels, ignoring the pronunciation of names. I digest what I want to take and throw the rest away. I experiment; I walk away with ideas quite contrary to the intentions of the original author, but those ideas become quite active in my rethinking of the direction of my life. Reading for the other self can be sloppy, systematic, or involve large amounts of rereading. No one knows and I don't care. There is a lovely cloak of anonymity that protects me. When I read for me, I am usually "right" in my unilateral understanding of texts. I can be reckless, brilliant, experimental, and delighted with the richness of authors, characters, and the language I meet on the page. Would that the same luxury could be afforded many of our young writers, who must share all of their written texts with teachers and groups.

Professional writers hide their drafts, withhold most of their junk, keep old stuff in boxes and file cabinets. They choose what the world will see. Their experiments or wild thoughts at three in the morning never reach public audiences. We may be missing out on some superior development in young writers who may need to withhold more of their writing experiments than we permit them. On this score, we may be doing a better job in allowing our children to experiment with texts in reading. If given the space, young readers can experiment and grow just as the professional does in his writing.

There is a historical side to the other self that can rise up out of the unconscious like the whale, Moby Dick. I find that the historical self, for me and for other readers, pops in when an external audience becomes involved. The other day I was reading a poem I wanted to share with our research team and suddenly the other self was drawing on a history of forty years of university-driven anxiety about the interpretation of poetry. I was highly conscious of a self that was laboring with dictionary, line analysis, and a host of other audiences: my group, and the author of the text.

Another "other self" or "internal" audience is that of the author of the text herself. Occasionally I know the author personally, but most of the time I create an image of the person and have dialogue with that person about the piece she has written. In the classrooms where we are conducting research teachers take great pains to share photos of professional authors, their backgrounds, and the different texts they write. They want the children to realize that crafting persons worked very hard to come up with the text they ultimately put into hard cover. No doubt the author I often create is a fiction, sometimes an extension of myself; nevertheless, I am aware of a different text evolving because I created a person with whom I could have dialogue.

The Teacher

External Audiences

The teacher is traditionally the most important audience learners encounter in their school careers. From kindergarten through doctoral study, classrooms are structured that way. Most work in reading requires the student to read with a view to matching the resident professional's text. More authority rests with the teacher when the teacher is interpreting a third party's text, but experience shows that there is enormous diversity among teachers interpreting the same text. Thus, students are often required to come up with texts quite foreign not only to themselves, but also the original author of the piece.

The sad thing is that text interpretation of this type rules out the reader's voice, the child's own struggle with the text. Rather, the child attempts to read while looking over his shoulder, second-guessing his match with the teacher, rather than struggle with what he might take away for himself, or share with others.

The teacher's role in reading, as in writing, is to listen to the children's diverse interpretations, their attempts to "draft" their way into meaning. Teachers ask questions that send children back to texts, but above all, they learn to share their enjoyment of a hard won fact, the richness of dialogue, and the beauty of metaphor. They hold discussions connecting literature with the everyday life experiences of the children.

Nancie Atwell at the Boothbay Elementary School in Boothbay Harbor, Maine (see her chapter in this collection), conducts a running, written dialogue with her thirteen-year-old students to the tune of two thousand dialogues a year. She asks struggling students to read books she hasn't read, to help them establish their voices, their interpretations before they know she has established hers. Her students now write to each other in addition to Nancie; they gossip about literature and its relation to their lives today. These young teens each gossip their way through an average of thirty-five books a year.

The Interpretive Community

When teachers allow children to share their reading and writing, interpretive communities spring up that at first resemble those encountered in writing. That is, children tend to be rather boisterous in listening too much to the voices of other readers rather than their own. A kind of "group-think" can exist and the teacher has the same task: to stress the individuality of book selection, reading process, and interpretation of the text.

Teachers need to be sensitive to the place of the interpretive community and its effect on how children read. Thus, the teacher's task is to help children learn how to listen to the reading of others. The approach is virtually the same as in writing. The children receive what the child has read, making sure they have accurately heard what the child has read, and then they ask clarifying questions about process, understanding, and what struck the reader. A well-developed interpretive community leads to what I think is one of the most important, yet neglected, approaches to reading, namely the child-controlled audience.

Child-Controlled Audience

We have found that a high diet of child-chosen topics is very important to a child's development in writing. To a large degree, children have learned both to choose topics and to effectively shape material for first audience (self) and second audience (class community). Book choice and reader-selected audience can be even more exciting in reading than it is in writing.

How many times have you found yourselves in the midst of reading a selection, thinking part way through, "I know just who ought to read this"? From that moment on you produce a dialogical text that fits the contours of your friend's thinking and personality. It is not unlike going to the cinema with a friend and producing two texts, one for you and one for your friend, knowing that you'll discuss the film over coffee afterwards. Even more exciting is going to a particularly good film with three different persons on three occasions. Once again, the text will be quite different depending on the person you are with.

We find that children enjoy reading when they can share their books with a self-selected audience. They know the children who like Beverly Cleary, S. E. Hinton, or Madeline L'Engle, horses, mysteries, or science fiction. If children are surrounded with literature, and helped to help each other, the best kind of audience use goes on when children can choose their audiences through informal sharing at all stages of their reading.

Sadly, most of our teaching of reading provides but one audience, the teacher. Even worse, the material children have to read in most controlled reading programs doesn't provide material the children would ever want to discuss or test on other audiences. The reading structure is simple: read, comprehend and answer teacher questions. The child knows the teacher will check his answers against answers already published in her manual.

Reading programs that provide limited audience, fill-in-the-blank responses to teachers alone, bypass the most important part of the reader, the other self. Children read and continually deny that part of self that would steal away with different interpretations, different applications to life itself. A child may delight in trivia not included in a lesson and never be able to share it. We want readers with voices, who can discuss or gossip about books with the teacher, peer groups, and self-selected classmates.

Too many of our children won't read unless they are part of a directed reading lesson. The issue is far greater than a skills problem. We continually bypass "the other self"—that part of the reader that shares with self and then with others. Both are inextricably intertwined. Reading is for discovery, delight, and for sharing with others. We need more news about readers doing just that.

References

Kennedy, X. J. "Little Elegy", *Nude Descending a Staircase*, N. Y.: Doubleday and Company, 1961.

Murray, Donald M. "Teaching the Other Self: The Writer's First Reader." *College Composition and Communication* 33 (May 1982): 145–147.

What Happens When Students Learn to Write

DONALD M. MURRAY

Students become writers when they read on their own page, in their own hand, what they did not intend to write. They watch—with fascination, with fear, with pride—as their own words sent forth to do one job, perform another. A text emerges as a print in a dark room rises from the paper, astonishing the observer, first pale shadow, then clear line, revealing to the photographer what the photographer, unknowing, saw. The writer's evolving text exposes the writer to the writer, the writer seeing, the writer thinking.

The student who was living one life becomes a writer and lives twice, thrice, a multiplication of lives, each life of words reassembling the lived life into new meanings. The text, moving away from the student's control, turns back to instruct the student, making meaning of what the student gathered, knowing and unknowing, living and studying. The evolving text, saying what it did not expect to say, passes back and forth over experience making new connections, contradictions, imaginings.

The student thinks and watches the student thinking, playing both creator and critic in the game of making meaning. The student writes to make use of what is being learned to explore the new learnings that appear, almost magically, in the draft.

Writing—writing that is working, writing like these lines which run ahead of the writer to chase their own meaning—always surprise the writer. And the student, becoming a writer, continually seeks new surprises, new meanings, new lives of words. Students who believed you thought, then wrote, now write to think.

This previously appeared in *The New Hampshire Times*.

Bibliography of Information Relevant to Topics in This Book

COMPILED BY RUTH HUBBARD

Altwerger, B. and Goodman, Y. "Reading—How does it begin?" In *Discovering Language with Children,* ed. G. S. Pinnell. Urbana, Ill.: National Council of Teachers of English, 1980.

Ferreiro, E. and Teberosky, A. *Literacy Before Schooling.* Portsmouth, N. H.: Heinemann Educational Books, 1982.

Harste, Jerome; Burke, Caroline; and Woodward, Virginia. *Language Stories and Literacy Lessons.* Portsmouth, N. H.: Heinemann Educational Books, 1984.

Hiebert, Elfrida. "Preschool Children's Understanding of Written Language." *Child Development* 49 (1978): 1231–34.

——————. "Developmental Patterns and Interrelationships of Preschool Children's Print Awareness." *Reading Research Quarterly* 16 (1981): 236–59.

Lamme, Linda and Childers, Nancye. "The Composing Process of Three Young Children." *Research in the Teaching of English* 17 (February 1983): 31–50.

Teale, W. H. "Toward a Theory of How Children Learn to Read and Write Naturally." *Language Arts* 59 (1982): 555–70.

Temple, Charles; Nathan, Ruth; and Burris, Nancy. *The Beginnings of Writing.* Boston: Allyn and Bacon, 1982.

Newkirk, Thomas. "Archimedes' Dream." *Language Arts* 61 (April 1984): 341–49.

Holdaway, Donald. *The Foundations of Literacy.* Sydney: Ashton Scholastic, 1979.

Wiseman, D. L. "Helping Children Take Early Steps Toward Reading and Writing." *The Reading Teacher* 37 (January 1984): 340–44.

Birnbaum, June C. "The Reading and Composing Behavior of Selected Fourth and Seventh Grade Students." *Research in the Teaching of English* 16 (October 1982): 241–60.

Birnbaum, June and Emig, Janet. "Creating Minds, Created Texts: Writing and Reading." In *Developing Literacy,* ed. Robert Parker and Frances Davis. Newark, Del.: IRA, 1983.

Bissex, Glenda. *GYNS AT WRK: A Child Learns to Write and Read.* Cambridge: Harvard University Press, 1980.

Blackburn, Ellen. "Common Ground: Developing Relationships Between Reading and Writing." *Language Arts* 61 (April 1984): 367–75.

Literacy Before School

Writing and Reading

Boutwell, Marilyn. "Reading and Writing: A Reciprocal Agreement." *Language Arts* 60 (September 1983): 723–30.

Bruffee, Kenneth. "Writing and Reading as Collaborative or Social Acts." In *The Writer's Mind: Writing as a Mode of Thinking,* ed. Janice Hays, Phyllis Roth, Jon Ramsey, and Robert Foulke. Urbana, Ill.: National Council of Teachers of English, 1983.

Cioffi, Grant. "Observing Composing Behaviors of Primary Age Children: The Interaction of Oral and Written Language." In *New Directions in Composition Research,* ed. Richard Beach and Lillian Bridwell. New York: Guilford Press, 1984.

Chomsky, Carol. "Write First, Read Later." *Childhood Education* 47 (1971): 296–99.

——————. "Approaching Reading Through Invented Spelling." In *Theory and Practice of Early Reading,* vol. 2, ed. L. B. Resnick and P. A Weaver. Hillsdale, N. J.: Lawrence Erlbaum, 1979.

D'Angelo, Frank. "Luria on Literacy: The Cognitive Consequences of Reading and Writing," In *Literacy as a Human Problem,* ed. James C. Raymond. Tuscaloosa, Ala.: University of Alabama Press, 1982.

DeFord, Diane E. "Literacy: Reading, Writing, and Other Essentials." *Language Arts* 58 (September 1981): 652–58.

Flower, Linda and Hayes, J. R. "The Cognition of Discovery: Defining a Rhetorical Problem." *College Composition and Communication* 31 (1980): 27–43.

Forester, A. D. "What Teachers Can Learn from Natural Readers." *The Reading Teacher* 31 (1977): 160–66.

Goelman, H., Oberg, A., Smith, F., eds. *Awakening to Literacy.* Victoria: Heinemann Educational Books, 1984.

Graves, Donald H. *A Researcher Learns to Write.* Portsmouth, N. H.: Heinemann Educational Books, 1984.

Graves, Donald and Hansen, Jane. "The Author's Chair." *Language Arts* 60 (February 1983): 176–83.

Hansen, Jane. "First-Grade Writers Who Pursue Reading." In *fforum revisited,* ed. P. Stock. Montclair, N. J.: Boynton/Cook, 1983.

——————. "Authors Respond to Authors." *Language Arts* 60 (Nov/Dec. 1983): 970–76.

Heath, Shirley Brice. "The Functions and Uses of Literacy." *Journal of Communications* 30 (Winter 1980): 123–33.

Hjelmervik, Karen and Merriman, Susan. "The Basic Reading and Writing Phenomenon: Writing as Evidence of Thinking," In *The Writer's Mind: Writing as a Mode of Thinking,* ed. Janice Hays, Phyllis Roth, Jon Ramsey, and Robert Foulke. Urbana, Ill.: National Council of Teachers of English, 1983.

Hogart, R. "The Importance of Literacy." *Journal of Basic Writing* 3 (1980): 74–87.

Jensen, Julie, ed. *Composing and Comprehending.* Urbana, Ill.: National Council of Teachers of English, 1984.

Jazemek, Francis E. "'I wanted to be a Tencrs to help penp to I———': Writing for Adult Beginning Learners." *Journal of Reading* 27 (April 1984): 614–19.

Langer, Judith and Smith-Burke, M. Trika, eds. *Reader Meets Author/ Bridging the Gap* Newark, Del.: IRA, 1982.

Murray, Donald M. "What Makes Readers Read?" *English Journal* 68 (May 1979): 69.

——————————. "Teacher the Other Self: The Writer's First Reader." *College Composition and Communication* 23 (May 1982): 140–47.

Petrosky, Anthony. "From Story to Essay: Reading and Writing." *College Composition and Communication* 33 (February 1982): 19–36.

Read, Charles. "Writing Is Not the Inverse of Reading for Young Children." In *Writing: Process, Development, and Communication,* vol. 2, ed. C. Frederickson and J. Dominic. Hillsdale, N. J.: Lawrence Erlbaum, 1981: 105–15.

Rubin, Andee and Hansen, Jane. "Reading and Writing: How are the First Two 'R's' Related?" In *A Decade of Reading Research: Implications for Practice,* ed. J. Orasanu. Hillsdale, N. J.: Lawrence Erlbaum, 1985.

Samuels, Marilyn S. "Norman Holland's 'New Paradigm' and the Teaching of Writing." *Journal of Basic Writing* (Winter, 1978): 52–61.

Shanahan, Timothy. "Nature of Reading-Writing Relation: An Exploratory Multivariate Analysis." *Journal of Educational Psychology* 76 ·(June 1984): 466–77.

Taylor, Denny. *Family Literacy: Young Children Learning to Read and Write.* Portsmouth, N. H.: Heinemann Educational Books, 1983.

Tierney, Robert J. and LaZansky, Jill. "The Rights and Responsibilities of Readers and Writers: A Contractual Agreement." *Language Arts* 57 (September 1980): 606–13.

Troyka, L. Q. "The Writer as Conscious Reader." In *Building Bridges Between Reading and Writing,* ed. M. Sternglass and D. Buturff. Conway, Ala.: L & S Books, 1981.

Yoos, G. "An Identity of Roles in Writing and Reading." *College Composition and Communication* 30 (1979): 245–49.

Development

Applebee, Arthur N. *The Child's Concept of Story: Ages Two to Seventeen.* Chicago: The University of Chicago Press, 1978.

Black, Janet. "Are Young Children Really Egocentric?" *Young Children* 36 (September 1981): 51–55.

Clay, Marie M. *What Did I Write?* Aukland: Heinemann Educational Books, 1975.

Dyson, Ann Haas. "The Role of Oral Language in Early Writing Process." *Research in the Teaching of English* 17 (February 1983): 1–30.

Donaldson, Margaret. *Children's Minds.* Glasgow: William Collins and Son, 1978.

Grinell, Paula and Burris, Nancy. "Drawing and Writing: The Emerging Graphic Communication Process." *Topics in Learning and Learning Disabilities* 3 (October 1983): 21–31.

King, M., and Rentel, V. "Toward a Theory of Early Writing Development." *Research in the Teaching of English* 13 (1979): 243–53.

Miller, George. *Spontaneous Apprentices: Children and Language.* New York: Seabury Press, 1977.

Schwartz, Judith. "Children's Experiments with Language." *Young Children* 36 (July 1981): 16–25.

Classrooms

Barenbaum, Edna. "Writing in the Special Class." *Topics in Learning and Language Communication* 3 (October 1983): 12–20.

Bartholomae, David. "Teaching Basic Writing: An Alternative to Basic Skills." *Journal of Basic Writing* (Spring 1979): 85–109.

Berger, Allan and Robinson, Alan. eds. *Secondary School Reading: What Research Reveals for Classroom Practices.* Urbana, Ill.: National Council of Teachers of English, 1983.

Branscombe, A. "Giving Away My Classroom: Teacher as Researcher." In *Teacher as Researcher,* ed. D. Goswami and L. Odell. Sharon, Conn.: Boynton/Cook. In Press.

Butler, Andrea and Turbill, Jan. *Toward a Reading/Writing Classroom.* Rosebury, Australia: Primary English Teaching Association, 1984.

Calkins, Lucy. *Lessons from a Child.* Exeter, N. H.: Heinemann Educational Books, 1983.

Cohn, Margot. "Observations of Learning to Read and Write Naturally," *Language Arts* 58 (May 1981): 549–56.

Dionisio, Marie. "Write? Isn't this Reading Class?" *The Reading Teacher* 36 (April 1983): 746–50.

Duffy, Gerald. "Fighting off the Alligators: What Research in Real Classrooms Has to Say about Reading Instruction." *Journal of Reading Behavior* 14 (1982): 357–72.

Dyson, Ann Haas. "Reading, Writing, and Language: Young Children Solving the Written Language Puzzle." *Language Arts* 59 (November/December 1982): 829–39.

Flores, S. "The Problem of Dead Letters: Social Perspective on the Teaching of Writing." *Elementary School Journal* 80 (1979): 1–7.

Forester, A. D. "What Teachers Can Learn from Natural Readers." *Reading Teacher* 31 (1977): 160–66.

Galda, Lee. "The Relations Between Reading and Writing in Young Children." In *New Directions in Composition Research,* ed. Richard

Beach and Lillian Bridwell. New York: Guilford Press, 1984: 191–204.

Galda, Lee. "Teaching from Children's Responses." *Language Arts* 59 (February 1982): 137–42.

Golden, Joanne M. "Children's Concept of Story in Reading and Writing." *The Reading Teacher* 37 (March 1984): 578–84.

Groff, Patricia. "Children's Oral Language and Their Written Composition." *Elementary School Journal* 78 (1978): 181–91.

Harste, Jerome and Burke, Carolyn. "Examining Instructional Assumptions: The Child as Informant." *Theory into Practice* 19 (1980): 170–78.

Harste, Jerome C., Woodward, Virginia A., Burke, Carolyn L. "Examining our Assumptions: A Transactional View of Literacy and Learning." *Research in the Teaching on English* 18 (February 1984): 84–108.

Heath, Shirley Brice. *Ways With Words: Ethnography of Communication, Communities, and Classrooms.* Cambridge: Cambridge University Press, 1983.

Kantor, Kenneth. "Classroom Contexts and the Development of Writing Institutions: An Ethnographic Case Study." In *New Directions in Composition Research,* ed. Richard Beach and Lillian Bridwell. New York: Guilford Press, 1984: 72–94.

Martin, Nancy. "Genuine Communications." *Topics in Learning and Learning Communication* 3 (October 1983): 1–11.

Newkirk, Thomas. "Anatomy of a Breakthrough: Case Study of a College Freshman Writer." In *New Directions in Composition Research,* ed. Richard Beach and Lillian Bridwell. New York: Guildford Press, 1984: 131–48.

Rycik, James. "What, No Questions?" *Journal of Reading* 26 (December 1982): 211–13.

Tway, Eileen. "Teacher Responses to Children's Writing." *Language Arts* 57 (1980): 763–72.

Vukelich, Carol and Golden, Joanne. "Early Writing: Development and Teaching Strategies." *Young Children* 39 (January 1984): 3–11.

Other

Arnheim, Rudolf. "On Inspiration." In *Toward a Psychology of Art,* Berkeley, Calif.: University of California Press, 1972: 285–92.

Berthoff, Ann. *The Making of Meaning.* Montclair, N. J.: Boynton/Cook, 1982.

Britton, James. *Prospect and Retrospect: Selected Essays of James Britton,* Montclair, N. J.: Boynton/Cook, 1982.

Bruner, Jerome S. *On Knowing—Essays for the Left Hand.* Cambridge: Harvard University Press, 1979.

Bruce, Bertram. "What makes a good story?" *Language Arts* 55 (1978): 460–66.

DeVilliers, Peter and DeVilliers, Jill. *Early Language*. Cambridge: Harvard University Press, 1979.

Friere, P. *Pedagogy of the Oppressed*. New York: Seabury Press, 1968.

Goody, Jack. *The Domestication of the Savage Mind*. New York: Cambridge University Press, 1977.

Graves, Donald H. and Stuart, Virginia. *Write from the Start*. New York: E. P. Dutton, 1985 (in press).

Halliday, M. A. K. *Explorations in the Function of Language*. London: Edward Arnold, 1973.

Holland, Norman. *The Dynamics of Literary Response*. New York: W. W. Norton, 1975.

MacLean, Marion. "Voices Within: The Audience Speaks." *English Journal* 72 (November 1983): 62–66.

Murray, Donald M. *Learning By Teaching*. Monclair, New Jersey: Boynton/Cook, 1983.

Ong, Walter. "The Author's Audience Is Always Fiction." *Interfaces of the Word,* ed. W. Ong. Ithaca: Cornell University Press, 1977.

Papert, S. *Mindstorms*. New York: Basic Books, 1980.

Perrone, Vito; Miller, Florence; Haney, Walter; et al. "The Family Learning Guide to Standardized Tests." *Family Learning,* vol. 1 (September/October 1984): pull-out booklet.

Pinnell, Gay Su, ed. *Discovering Language With Children*. Urbana, Ill.: National Council of Teachers of English, 1980.

Rosenblatt, Louise M. "What Facts does this Poem Teach You?" *Language Arts* 57 (1980): 386–94.

The Schoolboys of Barbiana. *Letter to a Teacher*. New York: Vintage Books, 1971.

Thaler, Ruth. "Art and the Written Word." *Journal of Basic Writing* (Summer 1980): 72–81.

Vygotsky, L. S. *Thought and Language*. Cambridge: MIT Press, 1962.
——————. *Mind in Society*. Cambridge: Harvard University Press, 1978.

Reading

Allington, Richard. "The Reading Instruction Provided Readers of Differing Ability." *Elementary School Journal* 83 (May 1983): 548–58.

Billman, Carol. "The Child Reader as Sleuth." *Children's Literature in Education* 15 (1984): 30–41.

Britch, Carroll. "Through the Narrator with Word and Character." *College English* 43 (March 1981): 242–52.

Bruce, Bertram. "Stories Within Stories," *Language Arts* 58 (November/December 1981): 931–36.

Fish, Stanley. *Is there a Text in this Class?* Cambridge: Harvard University Press, 1980.

Fish, Stanley and Iser, Wolfgang. *The Implied Reader,* Baltimore: Johns Hopkins University Press, 1974 (particularly Chapter 11, pp. 274–94).

Iser, Wolfgang. *The Act of Reading: A Theory of Aesthetic Response.* Baltimore: Johns Hopkins University Press, 1978.

Jacobson, Mary. "Looking for Literary Space: The Willing Suspension of Disbelief Re-visited." *Research in the Teaching of English* 16 (February 1982): 21–38.

Lester, Julius. "The Beechwood Staff." *The Horn Book* 15 (April 1984): 101–69.

Le, Thao. "Cognitive and Metacognitive Aspects of Reading." *Language Arts* 61 (April 1984): 351–55.

McGillis, Roderick. "Calling a Voice out of Silence: Hearing What We Read." *Children's Literature in Education* 15 (1984): 22–29.

Ohanian, Susan. "Good Teachers Make Reading Come Alive." *Family Learning* 1 (September/October 1984): 62–67.

Rosenblatt, Louise. *The Reader, the Text, the Poem.* Carbondale, Ill.: Southern Illinois University Press, 1978.

——————————. "The Reading Transaction: What for?" In *Developing Literacy: Young Children's Uses of Language,* ed. Robert Parker and Frances Davis. Newark, Del.: IRA, 1983.

Slatoff, Walter. *With Respect to Readers: Dimensions of Literary Response.* Ithaca, Cornell University Press, 1970.

Tierney, Robert J. and Pearson, P. David. "Toward a Composing Model of Reading." *Language Arts* 60 (May 1983): 568–79.

Vaughn, Joseph. "One Child's Query About Reading Instruction." *Language Arts* 60 (November/December 1983): 987–89.

Writing

Berthoff, Ann, ed. *Reclaiming the Imagination: Philosophical Perspectives for Writers and Teachers of Writing.* Montclair, N. J.: Boynton/Cook, 1983.

Brannon, Lil and Pradl, Gordon. "The Socialization of Writing Teachers." *Journal of Basic Writing* 4 (Summer 1984): 28–37.

Golden, Joanne. "The Writer's Side: Writing for a Purpose and an Audience." *Language Arts* 57 (1980): 756–62.

Graves, Donald H. *Writing: Teachers and Children at Work.* Exeter, N. H.: Heinemann Educational Books, 1983.

Emig, Janet. *The Web of Meaning.* Montclair, N. J.: Boynton/Cook Publishers, 1982.

Dyson, Anne Haas, and Genishi, Celia. "'WhattaYa Tryin' to Write?': Writing as Interactive Process," *Language Arts* 59 (February 1982): 126–32.

Gersten, Leon. "Getting Kids to Write Independently." *English Journal* 71 (February 1982): 66–67.

Kroll, Barry. "Writing for Readers: Three Perspectives on Audience." *College Composition and Communication* 35 (May 1984): 172–85.

Long, Russell C. "Writer-Audience Relationships: Analysis or Intervention?" *College Composition and Communication* 31 (May 1980): 221–26.

McQuade, Donald. "Creating Communities of Writers." *Journal of Basic Writing.* (Summer 1981): 79–89.

Moffett, James. *Coming on Center: English Education in Evolution.* Claremont, N. J.: Boynton/Cook, 1981.

Newkirk, Thomas and Atwell, Nancie, eds. *Understanding Writing.* Chelmsford, Massachusetts: The Northeast Regional Exchange, 1982.

Newkirk, Thomas. "How Competent Are the Writing Competency Tests?" In *Literacy as a Human Problem,* ed. James Raymond. Tuscaloosa, Alabama: University of Alabama Press, 1982.

Perl, Sondra. "Understanding Composing." In *The Writer's Mind: Writing as a Mode of Thinking,* ed. Hays, Janice; Roth, Phyllis; Ramsey, Jon; and Foulke, Robert. Urbana, Ill.: National Council of Teachers of English, 1983.

───────────. "How Teachers Teach the Writing Process." *Elementary School Journal* 84 (September 1983): 19–44.

Scardamalia, M. "How Children Cope With the Cognitive Demands of Writing." In *Writing: Process, Development, and Communication,* ed. K. Frederikson and R. Dominic. Hillsdale, N. J.: Lawrence, 1981.

Slevin, James. "Interpreting and Composing: The Many Resources of Kind." In *The Writer's Mind: Writing as a Mode of Thinking,* ed. Hays, Janice; Roth, Phyllis; Ramsey, Jon; and Foulke, Robert. Urbana, Ill.: National Council of Teachers of English, 1983.

Smith, Frank. *Writing and the Writer.* New York: Holt, Rinehart, and Winston, 1981.

───────────. "A Metaphor for Literacy: Creating Words or Shunting Information?" In *Essays into Literacy.* Exeter, N. H.: Heinemann, 1983.

Turbill, Jan. *No Better Way to Teach Writing.* Roxelle, Australia: Primary English Teaching Association of Australia, 1982.

Wiseman, D. and Watson, D. "The Good News about Becoming a Writer," *Language Arts* 57 (1980): 750–55.

Teachers as Researchers

Atwell, Nancie. "Class-based Writing Research: Teachers Learn from Students." *English Journal* 70 (January 1982): 84–87.

Berthoff, Ann E. "The Teacher as Researcher." In Ann Berthoff (ed.), *The Making of Meaning.* Montclair, N. J.: Boynton/Cook, 1981.

Clay, Marie. "Looking and Seeing in the Classroom." *English Journal* 71 (February 1982): 90–92.

Goodman, Yetta. "Kid-Watching: An Alternative to Testing." *National Elementary School Principal* 57 (June 1978): 41–45.

Goswami, Dixie, *Studying Writing: A Teacher's Guide to Classroom Research.* Montclair, N. J.: Boynton/Cook, in press.

Graves, Donald H. "A New Look at Research on Writing." In *Perspectives on Writing in Grades 1–8,* ed. S. Haley James. Urbana, Ill.: National Council of Teachers of English, 1981: 93–116.

Murray, Donald M. "Write Research to be Read." *Language Arts* 59 (October 1982): 760–68.

Nixon, Jon. *A Teacher's Guide to Action Research: Evaluation, Enquiry, and Development in the Classroom.* London: Grant McIntyre, 1981.